"Kipnis delivers all t
scandal-voyeurism rec
of wit .
—JIM HOLT, AUTHOR OF *STOP M.*
PHILOS
...ORY AND
... JONES

"'Know thyself' the ancient Greeks commanded. Far easier commanded than obeyed, as Laura Kipnis demonstrates in this incisive, hilarious look at four exemplary modern American scandals. In ways as delicious and disturbing as the transgressions themselves, she tells us why we love this stuff."
—DANIEL MENAKER, AUTHOR OF *A GOOD TALK: THE STORY AND SKILL OF CONVERSATION*

"Who knew it could be worth revisiting national bad dreams like Linda Tripp's smile or Oprah's diets? Kipnis unpeels meaning the way Freud would have, if he'd had a sense of humor."
—JONATHAN ARAC, AUTHOR OF *IMPURE WORLDS: THE INSTITUTION OF LITERATURE IN THE AGE OF THE NOVEL*

"Not only is this enormous fun, it is also a very smart book, rich in insight and psychological truth. *How to Become a Scandal* probes into our self-destructive impulses and our delight when others play them out. . . . Very satisfying and rewarding."
—PETER BROOKS, AUTHOR OF *TROUBLING CONFESSIONS: SPEAKING GUILT IN LAW AND LITERATURE*

"How many times have you watched the latest scandal unfolding on TV and said, 'How could he be so stupid'? Laura Kipnis gives you the answer and, along with it, a theory of why scandal, like rock and roll, is here to stay."
—STANLEY FISH, AUTHOR OF *SAVE THE WORLD ON YOUR OWN TIME*

"In the future, historians will have to read *How to Become a Scandal* if they want to understand this bizarre century. Laura Kipnis writes about the central conflicts in our society, the great comedies of manners, with the profound wit and broad sympathy that we used to find only in ambitious novels."
—MICHAEL TOLKIN, AUTHOR OF *THE RETURN OF THE PLAYER*

Also by Laura Kipnis

Against Love:
A Polemic

The Female Thing:
Dirt, Sex, Envy, Vulnerability

Bound and Gagged:
Pornography and the Politics of Fantasy in America

HOW TO BECOME A SCANDAL

HOW TO BECOME A SCANDAL

Adventures in Bad Behavior

LAURA KIPNIS

Metropolitan Books
Henry Holt and Company
New York

Metropolitan Books

Henry Holt and Company, LLC

Publishers since 1866

175 Fifth Avenue

New York, New York 10010

www.henryholt.com

Metropolitan Books® and ® are registered trademarks of
Henry Holt and Company, LLC.

Library of Congress Cataloging-in-Publication data

Kipnis, Laura.

    How to become a scandal: adventures in bad behavior / Laura Kipnis. — 1st ed.

    p. cm.

Includes bibliographical references.

ISBN 978-0-8050-8979-0

  1. Deviant behavior. 2. Scandals. 3. Celebrities—Conduct of life. I. Title.

HM811.K57 2010

306.70973'09049—dc22

                                      2010005036

Henry Holt books are available for special promotions and premiums.
For details contact: Director, Special Markets.

First Edition 2010

Designed by Meryl Sussman Levavi

Printed in the United States of America

1 3 5 7 9 10 8 6 4 2

To my dad

CONTENTS

HOW TO BECOME A SCANDAL

INTRODUCTION

I have become a problem to myself.

—ST. AUGUSTINE, *Confessions*

Leakiness

Around the time the married governor of a populous north-eastern state resigned following humiliating revelations about high-priced call girls and secret wire transfers to offshore accounts to pay for them, a man I was having dinner with, an intellectual type who writes earnestly about political and cultural matters of the day in highbrow journals and erudite op-eds, said with much certainty, apropos these recent events, that any man who claimed he'd never been to a prostitute was lying. "Really?" I said, adjusting my expression into studied neutrality while speculating inwardly about what special services were required that he couldn't find anyone willing to perform gratis—after all, he wasn't bad-looking (though one also hears it said that men aren't actually paying prostitutes for the sex, they're paying them to leave afterward). While I can't claim to be someone who musters vast outrage about the existence of prostitution (the issue should be unionization), this admission still took me aback: for one thing, I barely knew the man; also the contention that "everyone does it" seemed miscalculated, since even if they do, they're not routinely confessing it to their female dining companions. Maybe he mistook me for the nonjudgmental type as I've occasionally written on what might be called "transgressive" subjects, which does sometimes lead people to share such things with me unbidden. This is clearly a mistake on their parts since I can be a bit of a gossip, not to mention the fact that I habitually stash revealing sociological tidbits like this one away in a mental filing drawer for possible use in as yet notional articles or books that I may eventually write, not being one of those scandalous nonfiction writers you keep hearing about who just make things up (or not usually), a subject we'll be getting to.

Presumably my dinner companion hadn't paused to consider the potential transmission routes of the implied self-revelation before dropping it into the conversation; most likely he wasn't *thinking* much at all, it just "came out"—after all, the amount of sheer unconsciousness on display in the average social interaction would definitely overload the capacities of any device invented to quantify it. In the absence of such a device, we have our internal cringe meters, which shrill more and more frequently these days, given people's predilection for confessing their grubby secrets to passing acquaintances or even complete strangers: on talk shows, in their umpteenth memoir, at twelve-step meetings—it's like a national compulsion. Which brings me to why I mention this conversation. Scandal and compulsive unbosoming have a distinct family resemblance when you think about it: people driven to publicize their secret desires, for shadowy reasons and regardless of their own best interests.

"No mortal can keep a secret. If his lips are silent, he chatters with his fingertips; betrayal oozes out of him at every pore." The author (no surprise) was Sigmund Freud, the world's great exponent on the art of self-betrayal, a topic that will prove relevant to our investigations. Notice how *viscous* he makes the whole thing sound: betrayal doesn't trickle or drip or bleed, it *oozes*, mucuslike (or worse). His point is that humans can't seem to help spilling unwitting clues all over the place about the mess of embarrassing conflicts and metaphysical anguishes lodged within, though the viscosity of the substance in question will interest anyone who's ever struggled to quash some delinquent libidinal urge—presumably this would be everyone. The fact is that people are leaky vessels in *every* sense, which seems like a good starting point for a book on the subject of scandals, or, more specifically, certain people's proclivity for getting into them.

Of course, it's not like they're getting into them alone.

Other people's massive public self-immolations are their problem, obviously, but we all live in society together and the boundaries between people are spongy, with the messy needs and inner lives of complete strangers colliding and intermingling in the murky intervenient "space" that scandal opens up. Someone decides to act out his weird psychodramas and tangled furtive longings on a nationwide scale, playing out his deepest, most lurid impulses, flamboyantly detonating his life—it's like free public theater. The curtain opens on a bizarre private world of breached taboos, chaos, and misjudgment; through some brew of inadvertency or compulsion or recklessness, an unspeakable blunder is brought to light. And who's the audience for these performances? All the rest of us: commenting on the action like a Greek chorus, dissecting motives like amateur psychoanalysts, maybe nervously pondering our own susceptibilities to life-wrecking inchoateness, at least that's where my mind instantly goes.

Take the abovementioned governor. Previously a crusading attorney general with a reputation for sanctimony and moral fervor—including prosecuting prostitution rings, including signing a landmark anti-sex-trade bill raising penalties for men caught patronizing prostitutes (as he himself would soon be)—he'd reportedly forked over some $80,000 on secret trysts at upward of $3,000 a pop. The resignation came amid threats of prosecution and impeachment, announced at a mortifying press conference during which he admitted to "private failings," accompanied by a miserable-looking wife draped in Hermès, valiantly bent on keeping up appearances though that ship had clearly sailed. It was a pretty gruesome scene, like watching someone swallow a hand grenade in real time, which obviously didn't impede anyone's enjoyment of the event. Speculation abounded regarding the couple's sleeping arrangements, past, present, and future. A right-wing radio host blasted the wife for not seeing to the governor's "needs," earnest op-ed columnists speculated about the governor's inability to really *connect* with another person, the late-night comedians

had a field day ("To be fair, he did bring prostitution to its knees—one girl at a time"), a magazine cover displayed him in a full-length photo, an arrow pointing to his crotch labeled "Brain" . . . The projections flew like shrapnel.

My point is this. Scandals aren't just fiascoes other people get themselves embroiled in while the rest of us go innocently about our business; we all have crucial roles to play. Here is the scandal psychodynamic in a nutshell: scandalizers screw things up in showy, provocative ways and the rest of us throw stones, luxuriating in the warm glow of imaginary imperviousness that other people's life-destroying stupidities invariably provide. In other words, we need them as much as they need us. And speaking of that warm glow: if dancing on the grave of someone's shattered life and reputation weren't quite so gratifying, this would bode badly for the continuation of scandal, so it's lucky from scandal's point of view that other people's downfalls are as perversely fascinating as they are.

Please note that I speak as a scandal fan myself. I confess, I *love* these stories: the voyeuristic glimpses into the detritus of other people's lives, the quirky plot twists and emotional carnage . . . Who doesn't love them—as long as you're not the one stuck explaining to your spouse why you won't be going to work the next day and federal marshals are in the den seizing the home computer. Yes, I understand these people have done bad things, injured those who love them and torpedoed their lives in lavishly stupid ways, but clearly such impulses aren't their problem alone. It's the universal ailment if, as appears to be the case, beneath the thin camouflage of social niceties lies a raging maelstrom, some unspeakable inner bedlam. Scandals are like an *anti*-civics lesson—there to remind us of that smidge of ungovernability lodged deep at the human core which periodically breaks loose and throws everything into havoc, leading to grisly forms of ritual humiliation and social ignominy, or these days worse, since once the media get into the act, some of these poor chumps start looking more like bleeding open sores than actual humans, as gouged and disfigured as Old Testament lepers. Let's not forget, all joking aside, that society can get vengeful when you spit on its rules, otherwise known as the Reality Principle. Also that a certain amount of nasty glee on our parts *is* an indispensible element of scandal.

Blind Spots

Scandal watching may be our national spectator sport (or addiction), but despite the vast amount of cultural real estate it occupies, we lack any real *theory* of scandal. There's no scandal philosophy or psychology or ethnography: intellectually speaking it's pretty much virgin terrain when it comes to the meaning of scandal. In fact, the paucity of scandal theory is itself one of the interesting characteristics of the subject, whose structure and function it will be our task to reveal, like latter-day Darwins in the Galapagos of human peccadillo, wading into the muck, specimen jars in hand.

Certain subjects resist the interpretation they necessitate, it's sometimes said; especially when unconsciousness lies at the heart of things, there's an inherent slipperiness in the process. Nevertheless, theorizers begin by observing patterns, so let's start with the basics. Who *are* these scandal protagonists? Actually, it turns out you don't have to be a celebrity or in politics, contrary to general assumptions: even the most previously nonnoteworthy member of society can bring his life crashing down like the *Hindenburg* or a ton of substandard bricks with a little effort—less effort than ever in these fast-moving digitally driven times when anyone's innocent or not-so-innocent misstep can be beamed to computer and cell phone screens across the planet in a matter of seconds. I'm not saying that social position is entirely irrelevant for purposes of scandal-making; obviously the higher placed you are on the social ladder the longer the fall and the more likely the media will be camped out on your lawn when you land: scandal is always a complicated algorithm of prior social status, the particulars of the violation involved, and what else is happening in the news cycle at the time. If you're a celebrity in a murder case, hope that war breaks out the same day your trial begins; similarly, if you're a small-town mayor laboring under the impression that those lusty thirteen-year-old girls on the Web dying to meet you for ice cream sundaes and share naked pictures of themselves aren't undercover cops, here's some free advice: try not to get arrested on a slow news day.

Eminence and scandal are both locations on the social hierarchy, though inversely related: eminence is the social movement upward, scandal the trip back down. Recall Lytton Strachey's deliciously acerbic *Eminent Victorians*, a dissection of the era's hypocrisies, seen through the lives of the illustrious. Of course, the lives of the scandalous can be just as instructive, just as revealing of a cultural moment. Among the reasons Strachey comes to mind, one is that eminence and scandal are something of a closeted couple though, with all deference to the sublime Strachey, eminence is clearly the pantywaist of the two, as scandal is always delighted to reveal. Eminence only exists at scandal's mercy, forever haunted by its threat, since there lurks scandal sniffing at the back door, nosing around for cracks in the façade. Find one and *splat*, down goes another eminence, crashing to social ruin.

Speaking of closeted couples, this brings us to the exposer-exposee dynamic, which occupies a place of honor in the story of scandal. As you'd expect, Freud himself had a thing or two to say about the pleasure in uncovering other people's secrets, though it hardly takes the inventor of psychoanalysis to point out that the dedication of the exposé-minded to their endeavors can have a suspiciously driven quality.* Exposé is obviously a necessary component in the scandal-formation process, hinging as it does on dirty laundry aired and things "coming out," though tread carefully here, since exposers risk contamination themselves—note that no one really uses the word *scandalmonger* admiringly. Which may be another reason there's been so little written on the scandal dynamic to date: the risk of pollution by association.

It's not as though the pleasures of exposé aren't frequently cloaked in lofty-sounding motives, but that doesn't necessarily change the complexion of the enterprise. Let's say I went around exposing my previously mentioned dinner companion's name, on my blog (if I had one) or in a national magazine, to make an "example" of him. I suspect this might cause a minor ripple—not just his veiled self-revelations but the combination of malice and moral self-righteousness that my exposing him would inadvertently expose about me. Needless to say, the public sphere is awash in such unexamined motives,

---

*For the origins of this driven quality, see Freud on the "primal scene," in other words, what your parents were really up to when the bedroom door was closed (or worse, *ajar*), a fundamental childhood enigma that continues to ripple through adult consciousness in not entirely conscious formulations—for instance, the ardor to unlock sexual secrets and mysteries (or read about them in the tabloids). In fact, childhood sexual curiosity, namely the "Where do babies come from?" question, might be considered the prototype for all later forms of intellectual inquiry.

in fact it's a veritable lagoon of them. A few years ago, a well-known feminist writer caused a mini-scandal by publishing a lengthy diatribe in a national magazine accusing a particularly high-minded and much-revered literary critic of having groped her thigh some twenty years earlier when she'd been his student; she definitely came off worse than he did, despite claiming only the loftiest of intentions. Had she not foreseen that this would be the case? Apparently not: so consumed was she with the zeal to right an ancient injury that she was oblivious to everything else, from the ambiguity of her motives to the likelihood of ensuing ridicule. Which brings us to the *blind spot*, a location of particular interest to the scandal theorist.

Blind spots are the rabbit holes of scandal. They come in a range of models, from mini to deluxe, and we all have them, a little existential joke on humankind (or in some cases, a ticking time bomb) nestled at the core of every lonely consciousness. Compounding the situation, it's impossible to know precisely where they are, or other relevant data—diameter, fallout potential—since how can you see what you're blind to in yourself? If you could, it wouldn't be a blind spot and wouldn't trigger the various episodes of distorted logic and failed self-knowledge that occasionally snowball into the tortured little episodes we call scandals. You'd think it would require a rather sizable pair of mental blinkers to blot out the fundamental tenets of social existence and voluntarily transform yourself into a national laughingstock, exploding your life like a piñata for everyone else's amusement, yet despite the glaring disincentives, a sufficient number of people seem to keep managing it on a regular basis, thus keeping the scandal enterprise afloat (thankfully).

Recall the amorous governor, breaking laws he himself had helped put on the books. If there were a Nobel Prize for denial, Stockholm would soon be calling. The most popular diagnosis of the governor's condition was "hubris," shorthand for the proposition that the governor knew exactly what he was doing, had gauged the potential consequences and risks, effected a rational computation that he could get away with the transgression, and simply *miscalculated*. But let's consider a competing explanation, which proposes that one part of consciousness can be completely inaccessible to another part and this is basically the way the psyche is structured. The resistance to "compartmentalization"—a term popularized during the Clinton years when Americans were forced to account for a head of state acting with what seemed like an astounding amount of recklessness, including hairsplitting to the point of perjury—is understandable. If states of cognitive blockage are indeed commonplace, if otherwise shrewd and purposeful citizens can be simultaneously afflicted with an inner imperative to bring their lives crashing down around themselves while entirely oblivious to the possibility, then who's so confident that they're the master or mistress of every hidden proclivity or that every potentially ruinous desire is safely under lock and key and not at this very moment deviously tunneling for freedom? The premise that a significant percentage of the species resides in such states of self-incomprehension is alarming, especially to anyone still clinging to the classical picture of the self as rational and integrated, in the reassuring Cartesian fashion. (Of course, the idea that we're creatures who wholly understand our motives and stroll through life in a correspondingly self-coherent fashion would appear to be a symptom of compartmentalization in itself.)

If compartmentalization does indeed define the structure of the psyche, what an unlovely paradox we find ourselves saddled with, here in what's known as the human condition. And this is precisely what scandal keeps exposing: a rotating cast of characters whose mental lives seem to have been specially designed to thwart and defeat them; people not entirely unlike *us*, brought down by nothing less than their deepest selves.

Blind spots—yes, they're an epidemic, afflicting audience as well as scandalizers, which probably helps explain the big show of shock and surprise each time a new scandal breaks. Come on, what's more routine than buttoned-up officials caught in steamy sex scandals and moralists who don't live up to their own moral codes? Yet every time it happens somehow it's a novelty—the talking heads convene, the bloggers go into overdrive, and the rest of us can't stop rehashing all the latest revelations. In the case of the governor, I couldn't help noticing (glued as I was to the TV and devouring every headline) that the same cliché was repeated in story after story: "Americans reacted with jaw-dropping disbelief." "It was a "jaw-dropping fall from grace." "The sound of jaws hitting the floor could be heard." So many jaws were dropping you'd think Martians had landed in Times Square. What form of collective amnesia was afflicting the populace given that, not long before, the married governor of the adjacent populous northeastern state had also been forced to resign after equally humiliating sexual revelations (a gay affair), and in the interim there'd been at least a dozen exposés detailing various misadventures between congressmen, ministers, pages, interns, celebrities, hookers, and undercover cops, each replete with such giddy mistakes of judgment you had to wonder if they'd all been sniffing the same tube of glue.

The truth is that scandals invariably expose open secrets and things we already know: power corrupts, spouses cheat, capitalists are greedy, families can be seamy places—nothing all that surprising. But to the extent that scandalizers keep "forgetting" about social consequences, and scandal audiences keep "forgetting" about how routine such lapses are, this ability to both know something and not know it at the same time appears to be a common trait uniting these two ostensibly disparate groups. To wit—and here we come to our next theoretical bullet point—a capacity for *split consciousness* seems to be a trait we all share. And how convenient that we do, since minus this little pas de deux of forgetting and denial, how would scandal manage to do its job?

Watch Your Step!

Scandals aren't anomalies or marginal events, they're embedded in our collective lives; they may even be the marrow of collective life. Culture *needs* scandal, it's a necessary feature of the system, a social purification ritual, with the socially non-compliant branded and expelled, allowing the system to assert itself and its muscle. (What excellent public relations for toeing the line: get with those social norms . . . *or you're up next*.) Think of it as an unspoken sadomasochistic pact: scandalizers parade their irrepressible ids around in public, possibly even soliciting punishment (more on this to come), and the rest of us willingly deliver it—*thwack, thwack*—"Take *that*, you miscreant," like a big collective superego eager to disavow our capacity to wind up in a similar pile of shit one day ourselves. Yes, it appears we're the kind of people who enjoy watching other people "get what's coming"—probably not the most admirable trait in a population, but after all, it's *our* norms that are being violated. (Communities are enclaves of shared norms—scandals are what define a community.) The media may whip things up for motives of their own, but it's our standards that have to be breached, and we care about these breaches, deeply.

How could we not? Especially we who play by the rules: ours is the rage of bitter conformists. If we relish the lowered status of those kicked a rung or two down the social ladder, if we feel our self-esteem raised a notch or two as a result, this bears out what Kenneth Burke called the "hierarchical psychosis," the gassy brew of anxiety and envy fermenting in every social being's gut. Where do you rank, where do I, who has more (money, good looks, book sales)—those gnawing incessant social questions. The pleasure of knocking the excessively privileged and overly lucky down a notch or two can hardly be underestimated; what better outlet for *ressentiment* about your own middling station and fantasies about the good life and enmity toward those currently enjoying the good life but too spoiled to appreciate what they've got? Besides, who doesn't want *more,* more of something than they're socially entitled to? Who doesn't have embarrassing desires and intemperate appetites? Collective social life permits a few socially useful desires—major appliance purchases, monogamous marriage—and tries to quash the rest, that intractable little dilemma at the root of everything (see under: Civilization and Its Discontents). Maturity, willpower, self-control—sure, tout them all you want, right until they're wheeling you to your upstanding grave, but when *is* enough ever enough, especially when other people are getting more, as some of them invariably are, those fuckers, which is maddening in itself. Unlike the rest of the uptight social universe with its constricted little conventions and scarcity regimes, scandal *loves* your appetites, *all* of them, the more voracious the better.* Sex, love, money, ambition—scandal's playground all; add a dash or two of bad impulse control, sprinkle in some poor "self-management skills" or that well-fingered collection of grudges and narcissistic injuries, and suddenly along comes scandal, whistling its merry little tune: *"No one will know!" "It's our*

---

*When it comes to appetite, even the most quotidian form of insatiability—excess weight—can be scandalous. Recall Orson Welles, Marlon Brando, Elizabeth Taylor—all huge scandals, just for getting fat. A five-hundred-pound person who can't get through a doorway is usually a sufficient premise for a *National Enquirer* feature.

little secret." "Only chumps play by the rules." Fuck those bour-
geois prigs! says scandal with a wink, always the party animal. *Carpe diem! Take what's yours! Get even!* (Just don't get
caught, because then you're on your own.)

And thus does scandal lure its quarry. You can see how it
might happen—though obviously not to you or me, with our
vastly superior judgment and infinite self-knowledge.

But let your guard down for a second and . . . Needless to
say, lust has always been scandal's greatest pal, given that
funny way it has of occluding rational thought, particularly
when it comes to risk assessment; presumably this doesn't
come as news to any sentient being with the usual allotment
of sex organs and bottomless well of emotional hunger. But
appetite control alone won't forestall every disaster: what an
endless number of ways there are for anyone to wreck her life,
whatever her rung on the social stepladder. Who hasn't made
a potentially disastrous judgment call or two that could have
spelled ruination under the right confluence of circumstances:
seduced the wrong person (a high school student, a sibling),
"borrowed" funds or double-billed expenses, lifted a paragraph here and there (just kidding!), and yes, the definition of
"insider trading" *is* very confusing. Life is long, temptations
are many, and there's no shortage of material to stock the scandal coffers, human shortcomings being what they are: faking
résumés, faking scientific research, faking memoirs—scandal
loves unmasking a fake, making organized religion fertile
territory for obvious reasons. Then there's revenge, *la jalou-
sie*—a certain notorious ex–football hero comes to mind. Or

consider attachment, another of those nagging existential dilemmas—when to dig in, when to give up, when to run over your cheating husband with your Mercedes. And don't forget hypocrisy, routine though it is: what's more predictable than sanctimonious moralizing right-wing talk show hosts caught on tape offering to loofah their female employees (gently, in the "private" areas)? Still, it never fails to be of interest. The appearance-essence distinction is scandal's perennial motif; after all, everyone's hiding *something*. And topping the list there's self-delusion, which is as run-of-the-mill as ingrown toenails, and presumably to be human is to be on intimate terms with the condition, which can pave the path to your undoing, especially when compounded by sufficient quantities of miscalculation: *"They'll never find out."* (Of course they won't.) *"It seemed like a good idea at the time."* Usually it turns out to be rather less of a good idea in retrospect, from the Watergate break-in to shooting your married boyfriend's wife in the head. (Ineptly; she lives.)*

---

*Some scandals involve lawbreaking, though not all do; it's not a necessary condition. A president and a White House intern isn't a crime, at least if he manages to avoid perjuring himself about it. (Law belongs to the state, scandal belongs to the community.) Conversely, not all crime is scandalous. It depends on the type of crime and who commits it: a celebrity committing a minor crime is always a scandal, even if it's just shoplifting or punching someone out, while an ordinary criminal committing a crime generally fails to scandalize unless it's a particularly scandalous sort of crime—cannibalism, for instance. Castrating your sleeping husband is also usually good for a headline. Confusing the taxonomy further, celebrity murders tend to be treated more like entertainment than crimes, as are spouse-murders, particularly wives murdering husbands, who often get their own movies-of-the-week and become cultural icons. In short, the line between crime, scandal, and entertainment is currently rather ambiguous.

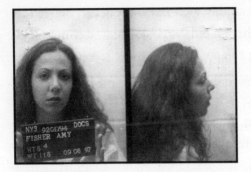

In other words, becoming a scandal is pretty much a piece of cake, especially these days. You don't even have to leave the house to wreck your life anymore: an accidentally misdirected lascivious e-mail can mean potential ruin once it's forwarded to thousands then picked up by the wire services, though let's be honest—was it really an accident? Self-sabotage is such an interesting subject and where would scandal be without it? It's occasionally been speculated that some collective universal guilt feeling underlies the human emotions, and this is one of the main emotional forces shaping our destinies, the curve ball of the human psyche. Is scandal the social face of such unlucky inner propensities? This question hovers in the background of our inquiries.

The Scandal GNP

Scandal may be a timeless subject, but we also live in particularly scandalous times. Scandal is one of the few reliable growth industries at the moment: scandal drives the news, scandal has merged with entertainment, scandal and the Internet are Siamese twins joined at the forehead. Hollywood scandals, tales of Celebrities Gone Bad blanket the culture—acrimonious divorces, late night DUIs, celebutante crack-ups. Even so, the immensity of the demand is such that supply can barely keep pace, what with all the tabloids and bloggers leeching off the daily payload. Hence the necessity to goose the process along at times, ferreting out dirt where there's dirt to be ferreted, inventing it when not. And what good sports they've been about it all, our celebs, tirelessly acting out for the cameras— throwing things at the help, shuttling in and out of rehab, turning up in homemade sex videos. The self-implosions of insecure personalities with grandiose tendencies: daily hay for the scandal mavens.

For the record, this isn't actually what I mean by "scandal." Don't get me wrong—obviously it's crucial to know what former-sitcom-actress-turned-movie-star is trying to pass off her nose job as surgery for a deviated septum and which leading man is too stupid to notice that the hooker giving him oral sex in the back of the limo is a transsexual with a contract to sell her story to the *Star* practically sticking out of her décolletage. But what's tedious about the glut of scandal-dependent industries and franchises is the insipid, mass-produced, mind-numbing product they're foisting on us, like everything else in modern life that was once robust and has now become industrialized and flavorless. What a lot of filler all this is—trivial dreck and trumped-up gossip passed off as "scandal" while fulfilling none of the essential conditions. A genuine scandal should have pathos and tragedy, it should have gravitas. It should jar our sense of social tidiness a little, it should incite unanswerable questions about human propensities and the moral compact and the ongoing battle between the anarchy of desire and the sledgehammer of social propriety. When I hear the word *scandal* I want shattered lives, downfall, disgrace and ruin, the rage of the community directed at its transgressors, not redemptive talk show moments and those insufferably arch "Best Scandals of the Year" lists each December.

The *real* best scandals, the most exemplary scandals, as with the cases that follow, are less digestible, more unruly—full of thwarted characters, convoluted plot points, and existential bad news. If Lytton Strachey had his Eminent Victorians, we have our Scandalous Americans: lovelorn astronauts and unhinged judges, malevolent whistle-blowers and over-inventive memoirists. Still, why these particular cases, why these protagonists out of all the possible candidates? Given the potentially limitless nature of the subject, I haven't tried to be either methodical or exhaustive—as Strachey warns, this is the path of tedium. Describing how he selected the four eminences to be put on his own dissecting table—a cardinal, a nurse, an educator, and a general—Strachey directs would-be social chroniclers to "row out over the great ocean of material, and lower down into it, here and there, a little bucket," bringing up some characteristic specimens to examine with careful curiosity. Forget being systematic; instead attack the subject in unexpected places, the flank or the rear: "shoot a sudden, revealing searchlight into obscure recesses, hither-to undivined." Adopt also a "becoming brevity."

Thus counseled, the scandals I've assembled here are characteristic specimens. Besides being small narrative gems, each of these cases is also completely paradigmatic. Each one represents a trouble spot in the social compact that no form of enlightenment or social progress seems likely to eradicate anytime soon: the revenge imperative, the flimsiness of rationality, the enduring stigma of ugliness, the hollowness of redemption—each one its own Waterloo of self-awareness, each another kick in the pants to the basic tenets of self-preservation. Such are the contradictions that structure our collective existence and punctuate everyday life. But to be candid, these scandals are basically the ones that leaped out and grabbed me, that made me squirm, that mortified and engaged and discomfited me at levels of my being I'd find impossible to spell out—what I'm trying to say is that they chose me as much as I chose them.

Part 1, "Downfalls," is about why they did it. Part 2, "Uproars," is about how we respond. All the stories are of the moment (at least of the last two decades), and all are variously notorious, although I've avoided the glitziest cases, which tend to become too encrusted with opinion to yield surprises. The focus is on individual scandals rather than the institutional variety, which are a different kettle of fish. These are contemporary tales, but note the classicism of the motifs: Crimes of Love, Madness, Enmity, Jealousy, Betrayal, Fatal Imprudence. As in the great tragedies, the human personality is helpless against itself: people orchestrating their own downfalls, crashing headlong into their own inner furies, the usual repressions and proprieties having somehow failed to do their job. But tragedy is supposed to concern noble feelings and high motives, while scandal is about ugly feelings and low motives, which are no less central and no less human. The trouble with scandal, essentially, is that it shows what really drives people. It reveals too much—everything we don't want to see and would prefer not to know, about them *and* us.

Hence the rock-hurling villagers, gnashing their teeth from the sidelines, savoring all the gory details of other people's disgraces in a happy fizz of moral indignation. Scandal may be an age-old public shaming rite, but its continued health and success depend on the vicariousness and malicious glee of all the rest of us, malicious glee that anyone who writes a book on scandal undoubtedly shares, for reasons both self-apparent and . . .

As I think I mentioned, failed self-knowledge *is* scandal's favorite theme.

PART I

DOWNFALLS

CHAPTER 1

THE LOVELORN ASTRONAUT

Crash Landings

If any one scandal in recent memory provides an illustrated manual in the art of leaking massive amounts of unconsciousness in public, it was the case of the "Celestial Love Triangle." Scandals come and go, but this one was like a gift from the gods to scandal lovers everywhere, though perhaps in a worrisome too-close-to-home sort of way for anyone who's ever been unceremoniously dumped then contemplated some kind of dramatic gesture in the feeble hope of rectifying things, not that I know anyone like that personally.

"Astro-Nut!" screamed the headlines. "Star-Crossed Space Cadet!" "Crazed Nutbucket!" As scandal narratives go, it was canonical, a masterpiece. If the essence of scandal is social downfall, Horatio Alger in reverse, nothing says downfall like the descent of a national icon. Especially one who'd been to space—you can't get much higher than that. And then caught in *diapers*, what more lacerating public shame? As someone deeply shame-prone myself, I always perk to attention when someone else is being put through the public shame machine; I imagine it's similar for any scandal aficionado. (According to psychologists who research schadenfreude, malicious glee at the misfortune of others is always greatest

 in areas of what they call "self-relevance.") The post-arrest pictures were grotesque: the once-feted lady astronaut looked like a lunatic—dark rings under her eyes, hair sticking out in every direction, a strange flush to her cheeks. What a contrast to the earlier shots of her prettily poised, waving and beaming in her orange bemedaled flight suit, a plucky heroine returning from a thirteen-day space jaunt as a mission specialist on the NASA shuttle *Discovery* just the summer before, a role model for young girls everywhere.

Needless to say, the before-and-after pictures ran everywhere, side by side, a graphic how-to in self-destruction and an invitation into the realm of human paradox (scandal's favorite hunting ground), where dualities run amok: where rationality and irrationality battle, love and hate contend, and the line between fantasy and reality can get tenuous. Every scandal perches on a scaffold of such antinomies, which is what gives them their dramatic arcs, their front-page potential.

The story went like this. On February 5, 2007, Captain Lisa Nowak, forty-three, a married mother of three, had been arrested at 4 a.m. at the Orlando International Airport, after driving all night from Houston to Florida, some 950 miles, in order to confront Colleen Shipman, a thirty-year-old air force captain who worked at the Launch Support Squadron at Cape Canaveral. Shipman was Nowak's alleged romantic rival for the affections of Captain William Oefelein, forty-two, a fellow astronaut whose NASA nickname was Billy O. Nowak was in disguise at the time, in a trench coat and wig. As if this weren't enough to propel the story into the headlines of every newspaper in the country and keep it there for weeks, the diapers did it. The police reported that Nowak had used diapers to pee in during her road trip so she wouldn't have to make pit stops; three used ones were found rolled up in a garbage bag on the backseat of her car. Follow-up stories helpfully explained that this wasn't as weird as it initially seemed since diapers are actually a familiar item for astronauts, who wear them during launchings and space walks when they can't get out of their pressure suits (who knew?), though NASA terminology for them is "urine collection devices."

As scandal prowls the land on the lookout for likely candidates, it's bound to be drawn to national heroes, but note the role that good props can play in the selection process. Diapers: what a brilliant piece of set design, speaking of leakiness. The great scandals often do have some iconic element that lingers on in the public imagination long past the shelf life of the scandal itself—recall Bill Clinton's cigar, Monica's thong, O.J.'s glove . . . We're symbol-using animals, foraging through whatever detritus the culture tosses our way to cobble together makeshift morality tales and life lessons, everyday tutorials on social normalcy. Clearly the diaper angle with its dual connotations of the geriatric and the infantile—neither especially flattering!—wasn't about to disappear anytime soon from the cultural landscape. It was just too good, the cringe-making high point of a supremely cringe-making story. The sadistic possibilities were too rich, and scandal would be nowhere without the pleasures of collective armchair sadism.

New scandals break out all the time, and the tale of the plummeting astronaut was soon succeeded by the next self-organized downfall, but the important thing to note about scandal in our time—and I mention this as a public service for anyone who may be on the verge of getting himself into one—is that the Internet is scandal's new best friend. Consider the grainy image of a distraught Lisa Nowak pacing back and forth and sobbing at the Orlando airport police station, as captured by the camera hidden in the ceiling of the holding cell where she was placed after her arrest. A uniformed cop who brings her a glass of water asks a few preliminary questions. "None of what you say is going to leave this room," he assures her, as recorded on the video footage now posted on the Web. Later that afternoon when detectives inquired of an obviously jittery Colleen Shipman, who'd just a few hours earlier been assaulted and pepper-sprayed by a strangely dressed woman in the Orlando airport parking lot, whether she'd ever heard her new boyfriend, Bill, mention the name "Lisa," and Colleen, trying to be helpful—for she *was* the helpful type, frequently apologizing for not remembering more precise details about her ordeal—replied that Bill *had* accidentally called her "Lisa" in bed recently, it's doubtful that she foresaw the day when the transcript revealing this salient bit of bedroom blundering would likewise be released and posted on the Internet, where it will probably remain for all of eternity. So that's the thing to remember about scandal these days: nothing ever goes away.

Before scandal snuck up and clubbed her over the head, Lisa Nowak hardly seemed like the kind of person who'd end up at the top of everyone's list for the most inexplicable public flameout of the year. Despite the high-profile career, she was actually pretty ordinary. She read mysteries and did crossword puzzles and had a standard-issue bad suburban marriage, living outside Houston with her husband, Rich, a flight controller at the International Space Station, though they'd recently separated after nineteen years. She'd been depressed and lost a lot of weight following the separation, both contributing factors, her lawyer would later argue, in her temporarily losing her marbles. Though Nowak had collected an impressive array of advanced degrees in highly technical-sounding fields and had been through Naval Test Pilot School, among the many things that surprised her co-workers at the Johnson Space Center when the scandal broke was that she'd somehow managed to navigate her way from Houston to Orlando by car—she was notoriously bad with directions. An astronaut with no navigational skills—it sounds like a bad midseason replacement sitcom premise. But what an ideal metaphor: Nowak *had* lost all sense of direction; some inner global positioning system had catastrophically failed. Whether humans are supposed to come factory-equipped with these devices or are responsible for acquiring one along the way (and who's to blame when yours suddenly gives out midcourse) were some of the larger questions hovering at the edges of this story.

Then there was Bill Oefelein, a former Top Gun pilot, handsome in that bullet-headed, all-American way and perfectly cast in the role of romantic pivot. Like Nowak, Oefelein had also been in long-term marital Siberia, in his case coupled to his former high school girlfriend, Michaella, though after sticking it out for seventeen years they'd split up a couple of years before. He told police that he and Lisa had been involved for the last two or three years but that he'd ended things once he met Colleen. It was unclear whether he and Lisa had been seeing each other during his marriage, and the police didn't press him on it (or not on tape). The relationship with Lisa had been "somewhat exclusive" for a period of time, though "nobody prohibited anything," as he put it enigmatically. She was one of his best friends at NASA, they'd had a relationship, and she was now an "ex" . . . but he hadn't really considered her his girlfriend, he

said, at least he'd never used the word. He sounds like a guy groping around to define something he hasn't entirely defined in his mind and is now being asked to spell out for a retinue of police, which can't be the world's most comfortable situation. Or maybe he just sounds like someone realizing a little late in the day that other people are largely unfathomable, one of those distressing facts of social and romantic existence that most of us have probably had to contend with at some point or another too.

Houston, We Have a Problem

Lisa told Chris Becton, the police detective who first interviewed her, that all she'd wanted was to talk to Colleen and to see what Colleen knew about her and Bill, but she was never going to *hurt* her. When asked if she thought squirting

Colleen with pepper spray was likely to advance a conversation, she admitted, "That was stupid"—sounding as though she'd just then realized it. The police had also caught Lisa with a compressed-air BB gun that resembled a 9 mm handgun (loaded with BB shot and its safety off), a steel mallet, a folding knife with an eight-inch blade, four feet of rubber surgical tubing, and lawn-size garbage bags. The BB gun was just to get Colleen to talk to her, but she'd never have used it, she never even had it out. Her explanations for the other items were not entirely coherent; in fact, she seemed a little baffled by their existence, as though someone had planted them on her or they'd dropped from the sky. When the police eventually searched her car, parked at a nearby motel, they found more pepper spray, cartridges for the BB gun, latex gloves, MapQuest directions from Houston to Orlando that had been printed out two weeks before, copies of e-mails from Colleen to Bill, and hand-drawn directions to Shipman's house (including longitude and latitude, in case she decided to get there by space shuttle). And those fateful diapers. Since Nowak had used a false name at the motel, paid cash, and had numerous deadly weapons in her possession, the police decided they had enough for an attempted murder charge.

And now comes the question on all of our minds: *What on earth was she thinking?* That this bungled attack on Colleen would win Bill back? That she wouldn't get caught, exposed, and nationally humiliated? As with every major scandal, there were enigmas aplenty, and it's the scandal audience's task to piece together the incomplete, inconsistent, and illogical bits of data into a coherent narrative, filling in the gaps with projections and speculations of our own. One of the unacknowledged bonuses of scandal narratives is that they thrust us into unanticipated metaphysical and ethical discussions with one another about all the most pressing matters—free will, moral luck, the stranglehold of desire, the difference between right and wrong—topics that philosophers these days have turned into tedious abstractions but that the rest of us want a chance to converse about too. All scandals demand this participatory element, each of us constructing different accounts from the available facts, drawing on our respective experiences and temperaments—misanthropy versus generosity, track records of romantic disappointment versus romantic triumph—with plenty of room to embellish freely.

And speaking of embellishment: about those diapers. A few months after Nowak was released on bail (to what must have been an entirely fresh form of hell) and the astronaut love triangle was still a hot item in every media outlet and raw-enough meat in the blood-spattered jungle of opinion and judgment that comprises the blogosphere, her large, blustery lawyer, Don Lykkebak, held an irate press conference to set the record straight. Nowak had *not* driven nonstop, he rebuked the assembled reporters, she'd spent the night at a motel along the way; the diaper issue was a "preposterous and scandalous story" fabricated by the police, spread irresponsibly by the media, and now Nowak would never get a fair trial because of all the diaper jokes. Predictably, the late-night comedians were still having the time of their lives, like a pack of jocular pit bulls with an injured lovelorn rabbit. Leno: "As you know, she went to court yesterday and was released on her own incontinence." Letterman: "So this woman astronaut drives nine hundred miles wearing a wig and a diaper. This is one giant step for man, one giant leap to the nuthouse." Leno: "And let me tell you something, ladies, nothing turns a man on more than a woman with a full diaper."

Who could blame them? Bathroom elements in public: always prime material for public shaming rites. Though according to Lykkebak, Nowak had no adult diapers in her car, just toddler-size ones that dated from a couple of years before, when Houston was evacuated ahead of Hurricane Rita and Nowak and her family (which included five-year-old twins), camped in the parking lot of a motel that wouldn't allow non-guests in to use the bathrooms, were forced to improvise solutions. Pressed by a clamor of skeptical questions, Lykkebak finally delivered an exasperated step-by-step account, in broadcast-tailored euphemisms, of exactly how someone might go about urinating into a diaper while in a parked car and attempting to maintain a semblance of privacy. The reporters tried hard to look serious, and Lykkebak tried hard to seem dignified, though you couldn't help thinking that Monty Python could have done a lot with this premise. In fact, nowhere in the interview transcripts does Nowak admit to peeing into diapers on her journey to Orlando. But if she hadn't, what was she doing driving around with used diapers in her car for two years, a hygiene-minded female reporter demanded of an increasingly sputtering Lykkebak, who seemed to take these questions as a personal affront, a technique that criminal defense lawyers presumably cultivate. Despite Lykkebak's best efforts, the issue wouldn't go away: if Nowak wasn't a diaper-wearing nut she was definitely some other kind of nut, and a slovenly one at that.

Whatever the truth about the diapers (and scandal details don't have to be *true* to be scandalous), they were a perfect symbol for falling afoul of social codes, for getting yourself in "deep shit" and winding up with your life "in the toilet"—given the wealth of such idioms, Nowak couldn't have found a better motif if she'd tried. (Or . . . had she? The unconscious has its own particular sense of humor, not to mention a potty mouth, or so it's been said; Freud wrote a classically unfunny book on the subject.) Real or invented, the diaper issue brilliantly distilled the scandalizer's situation to its essence, since what's an adult in diapers but someone whose self-management skills have critically failed?

Or to put it another way, self-management is what's supposed to keep us *out* of scandals, and this is our fundamental social task. Consider the massive amount of managerial labor that goes into achieving and maintaining even the most basic levels of social normalcy, given the thousands of minute rules governing the body alone, rules that have been pounded into all of us from the crib beginning with toilet training, everyone's introduction to socialization and the potential breach of which provides all the most colorful metaphors for public humiliation (as anyone who's ever been a child and ever set foot on a playground knows firsthand). This is labor every normal citizen performs at every minute of every day, because even the smallest lapses can plummet hapless violators headfirst down the social ranks, leading to grisly forms of ritual shaming, despite the fact that the majority of these rules are unwritten and only ever articulated in the breach. Additionally, as everyone knows only too well, bodily control *can* be notoriously precarious at times, vulnerable to the grim realities of illness, aging, and the occasional bad oyster; yet even momentary surrender is potentially scandalous, and the more highly ranked you are the more ridiculous your body becomes. When the first President Bush threw up on Japanese prime minister Kiichi Miyazawa during a 1992 state dinner in Tokyo, what a scandal! Not only was it bandied about the news for months—how would it affect diplomacy between the United States and Japan, what about trade relations?—it lives on in the cultural memory to this day. In short, simply having a body is the first step on the road to becoming a scandal.*

This is distressing, which may be why one senses a certain agitation in the nonstop mockery aimed at the "Star-Crossed Space Cadet." What if self-sovereignty *isn't* always as secure

---

*Which is why the out-of-control body—classically, slipping on a banana peel—is such a comedic staple, though in postmodern comedy bodily shame itself has replaced the pratfall. A TV sitcom like *Seinfeld*, purportedly "a show about nothing" but frequently about the permutations of bodily shame, could build an entire episode around Jerry's being suspected of picking his nose in his car; in its successor, *Curb Your Enthusiasm*, Larry gets suspected of having an erection in wildly inappropriate circumstances, and so on.

as one would like? What if you go around assuming you're in the driver's seat, then suddenly find yourself en route to Orlando on a crackpot romantic mission or in a police lockup being read your rights? These are a few of the many dilemmas Lisa Nowak presents us with. How someone previously rational enough to pass the battery of psychological exams inflicted on trainees before they're admitted to NASA and blasted into outer space could suddenly become so deeply and flamboyantly *unscrewed* was an enigma the country pondered, and hastily deflected with a stream of lame jokes. "Houston, we have a problem" was the leading contender.

Houston, we have a problem. The jocularity made it far easier to ignore the pathos of the story, including the fact that plummeting astronauts have, after all, been a periodic source of national tragedy. The insistent levity surrounding Nowak's spectacular plunge feels a little forced when you recall the decade's other astronaut disasters, for instance, the 2003 explosion of the *Columbia* space shuttle, which killed three of Nowak's former NASA classmates and which, it was later reported, Nowak had taken particularly hard. One of her close friends was on board, and she'd spent a lot of time with the friend's now motherless son after the explosion. There was something unsettling about the relation between the two forms of downfall, just as something seemed a little off in the viciousness of the humor aimed at Nowak, in the determination to treat the episode as high comedy. No doubt every scandal is also a ledger of social anxiety, but this one vibrated with a particular unease.

Hideous Stains

Colleen had flown back to Orlando late Sunday night from Houston, where she'd spent the weekend with Bill. They'd met at a party in Florida in November, the week after Thanksgiving (it was now early February) and started dating, but since he lived in Houston and she lived in Orlando, dating involved a lot of traveling and the accompanying hassles. Predictably, not only did Colleen's return flight get in at 1 a.m., an hour late, but it turned out her suitcase had been lost too—the usual traveler's nightmare—though it was supposed to be on the next flight, so she decided to just hang around until it came. Which is why it was well after 3 a.m. by the time she went outside to catch the parking lot shuttle, which is where she first noticed the strange-looking woman who was also waiting there—strange because she seemed to be wearing multiple layers of clothes and glasses with weird red frames that looked like they were from the eighties. It was Florida and nobody wears layers. Somebody's gotta help this girl with her fashion sense, thought Shipman.

Colleen and Lisa had never actually met, but their lives had overlapped in some fairly intimate ways. When Colleen had landed in Houston the previous Thursday, Bill had picked her up at the airport and taken her back to his apartment, where she seemed to keep stumbling over annoying traces of Lisa. "Since when do you ride a purple bike?" Colleen queried Bill, who had two bikes stored in his bedroom.

He said it belonged to someone from his bike team, and when she asked who, he admitted it was Lisa's—they were training for a race together, so she was keeping it there. Colleen wanted to know if it was wise to keep Lisa's bike if they'd split up. She wasn't going to tell him to get rid of it, but it made her uncomfortable, it made her want to pull away from the relationship, because she was wondering if he'd really cut ties with Lisa. Bill said he'd get rid of the bike the next day, though he didn't actually get around to it. Then Colleen used Bill's computer to check her e-mail and saw that Lisa had done the same thing, since when she went to type her e-mail address into the fill-in field, Lisa's e-mail address came up. Bill admitted that yes, Lisa had sometimes used his computer.

After things had started getting serious between them, Bill had told Colleen all about the relationship with Lisa, but he'd insisted that it was over and that Lisa understood the situation. She was even happy for him that he'd fallen in love; at least that's how Colleen recalled Bill's account of the breakup. From Bill's point of view, that was as much as he needed to tell her—after all, they both had their pasts. In fact, the two of them hadn't known each other all that long before their relationship was catapulted into the national spotlight, especially since Bill had spent half of December in orbit as co-pilot on the twelve-day *Discovery* shuttle and in preflight quarantine before that. Colleen wanted to know if it was *really* over with Lisa—she didn't want some crazy lady showing up at her door trying to kill her!—and Bill assured her that it was, definitely. The detective taking Colleen's statement perked up at that point and asked why she'd talked about someone killing her. Was there some problem with Lisa that she was aware of? Colleen said no, no problems, but you know how these things go. For one thing, it was a relationship Bill and Lisa had kept under wraps, and who knew how Lisa really felt about Bill's breaking things off?

The night after Colleen arrived in Houston, she and Bill went to a horror movie called *The Messengers*, about hideous dark stains that keep reappearing on the bedroom wallpaper no matter how many times you scrub them away. Given what was to come, it was an uncanny entertainment choice. Obviously you can't ever entirely eliminate the stains of previous lovers either: around the house, on the wallpaper, in the bedroom—so it goes in serial monogamy and other varieties of romantic entanglement as practiced in our time. It was the next night that Bill accidentally called Colleen "Lisa" in bed, but they'd been out at a party and had a few drinks . . . For all that, Colleen had no doubt things were over between Lisa and Bill, at least that's what she told the detectives when they queried her. She repeated it twice for emphasis: *"No doubt."* It's a well-known axiom that anyone who says "No doubt" twice in a row has some doubts. If one thing is clear, it's that well before the parking lot confrontation these two women were in each other's imaginations, which isn't *invariably* a scandal waiting to happen, though when it comes to scandal geometry, the triangle is by far the most promising configuration.

I'm piecing this narrative together from transcripts of the

police interviews, by the way, since unlike so many of the protagonists in recent scandals who feel compelled to explain their motives lengthily in television interviews or their subsequent memoirs, none of the principals in this case has thus far gone public, with the exception of Lisa, who at a two-minute press conference, looking as tremulous and unstable as a vial of nitroglycerin, apologized to Colleen "for having frightened her in any way," read a platitude-laden statement ("The past six months have been very difficult for me, my family, and others close to me . . ."), and took no questions afterward.* The reticence was a futile gesture, since the press demanded and soon obtained the court documents (only Nowak's psychiatric evaluations were excluded), a thorough reading of which not only reveals great nuggets of personal data about everyone concerned, but is also guaranteed to inspire a quick review of one's own relationship-breakup behavioral excesses from junior high on—all DWDs ("dialing while drunk"), unannounced visits to an ex ("just in the neighborhood!"), drive-bys, Web-stalking, and so on—to assess the probability that at some future date an impromptu 950-mile road trip to rectify a romantic injustice or commit nighttime assaults on rivals real or imagined might suddenly seem like a great idea.

But how can you possibly know in advance what lengths you're capable of, in extremis or otherwise? As psychologist

---

*As Nowak's media consultant, Margaret Mackenzie, advises in her book *Courting the Media: Public Relations for the Accused and the Accuser,* "Apologize without accepting blame."

Herbert Fingarette points out in his rather alarming 1969 study, *Self-Deception*, it's not just that "spelling things out" to oneself is an acquired skill (like driving a car, as he puts it in a bit of *avant la lettre* irony given the episode under discussion) but that there can be overriding reasons to avoid doing it *and* to avoid becoming conscious that you're avoiding doing it. Additionally, as novelist J. M. Coetzee frets in a cautionary essay on "Confession and Double Thoughts," it's impossible to know whether the "truth" you discover in your occasional feeble attempts at self-examination is anything close to truth and not just some self-serving fiction, since the "unexamined, unexaminable principle" governing your conclusions "may not be a desire for the truth but a desire to *be a particular way*"—to seem rational and coherent to yourself, for instance. In other words, all the self-examination in the world isn't going to help anyone bent on self-deception or when one part of yourself is bent on deceiving another part of yourself, which is no doubt true of any of us at least some of the time. That's what having an unconscious means (and thanks for nothing).

Scandal protagonists who, unlike Nowak, do choose to retail their stories invariably have lengthy explanations or justifications for whatever they did or didn't do that propelled them into scandal's path; these explanations often even make a certain sense, or at least you see how they might in a hermetically sealed cognitive universe, i.e., the padded cell of your own imagination. But given the finely tuned equipoise between self-doubt and self-deception in the human psyche, how can *any* self-examination not be just an "endless tread-mill," as Coetzee puts it? Worse, how can you be sure that whatever's perverse within yourself isn't just *feeding* on itself, part of the same perverse pattern of self-delusion that's galvanizing you toward the self-betraying act in the first place, while simultaneously producing convincing ratio-nales for the self-destructive act or motive?

Given her stiff upper lip with Bill, Lisa was obviously gifted at public dissembling, though Bill doesn't sound like someone who delved too deeply either. According to him, he'd broken things off with Lisa around the beginning of January, telling her he wanted to be exclusive with Colleen. Lisa seemed "dis-appointed," Bill told the detectives, but she appeared to accept his decision—at least that's what he told himself. But Lisa still wanted to stay close and she kept calling him a lot on his cell, even daily—sometimes *more* than daily—and he started not answering her calls, which apparently didn't dissuade her. The messages she left were friendly, not hostile, the two of them were still training for a bike race in April and working out together at the gym, so in fact they continued to spend a lot of time in each other's company. (It later emerged that Lisa was also doing a certain amount of behind-the-scenes jiggering of their schedules at the space center to ensure they'd do their mandatory flight training sessions together.) Bill had always thought of Lisa as just a really nice person, levelheaded, non-emotional; he'd certainly always assumed she was stable—he'd never even seen her angry in all the years he'd known her. He doesn't make her sound like the world's most exciting girlfriend: the spitfire tendencies seem to have been suppressed until that fateful weekend. She was shy, a bit private—maybe that was the problem, he now reflected, that she didn't really have anyone to confide in. "We're all full of theories," he answered ruefully, when asked by the police if he had any theories about why she'd done it. But he'd never have predicted *this*. She'd even wished him a nice weekend earlier in the week, knowing that Colleen was coming to town, though by that point she'd already hatched the lunatic scheme to face off with her rival in Orlando.

Bill was certainly the trusting type: Lisa had keys to his apartment *and* knew the password to his computer, which he hadn't bothered to change after breaking up with her. She was carrying copies of Colleen's e-mails to Bill when she was arrested ("First urge will be to rip your clothes off, throw you on the ground and love the hell out of you," was the most-quoted line in the news reports), meaning that she had snuck into his apartment to do a little reconnaissance when he was out and lifted Colleen's e-mails from his computer. She'd also found flight details for Colleen's weekend trip to Houston lying on the coffee table and had gotten hold of Colleen's phone number, though Bill was sure that the only place he'd had it was on his cell phone. It turned out Lisa had gone through his phone bills and deduced which number was Colleen's from how often he dialed it. Bill had no idea Lisa had been in his apartment; he hadn't noticed anything amiss—either at his place or with Lisa herself.

Later he felt horrible and responsible: it was his fault for booking such a late flight for Colleen (he'd used his frequent flier miles), and he should have seen signs that something was off with Lisa. He flew to Orlando to be with Colleen as soon as he heard what had happened; she said she was freaking out and asked him to come, so he did. Bill was a stand-up guy, according to everyone he worked with; even his ex-mother-in-law said in press interviews that he was "wonderful," despite his having divorced her daughter. (She also seized the opportunity to get in a few digs at Lisa about her supposed role in the demise of Bill's marriage, though without quite coming out and saying there was an affair.) Feelings at work ran less positive when it came to Lisa, who rubbed some people the wrong way. The Johnson Space Center was a clubby atmosphere, and she struck a lot of her colleagues as standoffish—prickly and not particularly easy to get along with in situations where teamwork is called for, including in space, where she displayed "bad expedition behavior" according to a fellow astronaut. (One of the side benefits of getting yourself into a scandal is finding out what your colleagues *really* think of you.) And did the office mates suspect that Lisa and Bill had been an item for the past few years? Some had heard rumors or reported seeing them leave parties together, but everyone also knew that Bill now had a new girlfriend in Orlando, which can't have been fantastically pleasant for Nowak, though she made sure to maintain that preternaturally cheerful face.

"She Looked Really Crazy"

The strange overdressed woman on the airport shuttle that February night, who would of course turn out to be Lisa Nowak, got off the bus first, putting some type of hood up over her head. As Colleen neared her car, she spotted Lisa again because she seemed to be trailing her through the parked cars, five or six car widths away, but keeping abreast, which was totally spooking Colleen. Colleen started walking faster, taking bigger strides, and got her keys out. When she saw her car she hit the unlock button, threw her bag in the back and jumped in the front with her backpack, locking the door as fast as she could. She heard loud footsteps getting closer and closer, and suddenly Lisa's face was pressed against the window and she was trying to open the door and slapping the window with her hand, pleading with Colleen to help her. She was saying something about a boyfriend—that he was supposed to pick her up but he wasn't there, and could she use Colleen's cell phone? Colleen was thinking that nobody who wants you to *help* them is going to try to open your car door. She shouted through the window that her cell phone was dead, which was true. Meanwhile Lisa was begging Colleen to drive her to the parking office, but she looked really crazy, like she was on drugs. Colleen told her through the window that she'd go to the parking office and send someone back to help. She started the engine, but Lisa was protesting that she couldn't hear her, so Colleen rolled the window down a crack—or she tried to roll it down a crack but it was the automatic type that just keeps going—and as she was trying to put the window back up and plug her cell phone into the console, she looked up and as she did, Nowak squirted her with some kind of pepper spray through the crack in the window and started trying to shoulder her way into the car. Her eyes burning, Colleen managed to close the window, put the car in gear, and hit the gas, leaving Lisa behind. At the parking office, the attendant gave her some paper towels to wipe her face—her skin too was burning now—and called the police and paramedics.[*]

Shortly afterward, the police picked up Lisa after spotting her tossing a white plastic bag into a trash can, which turned out to contain a black wig and the BB gun. In the duffel bag she was still carrying they found her nefarious arsenal—the mallet, rubber tubing, garbage bags—as well as $600 in cash and a pair of glasses with clear lenses. There was also a handwritten list with checked-off items—the things in the duffel bag and others that would later be found in her car. Lisa may have lost her grip, but at least she was being methodical about it.

After paramedics flushed out Colleen's eyes, police drove her over to where Lisa was being held. Colleen identified her

---

[*]The question of whether Shipman was actually hit *in* the face with the pepper spray would turn out to be a decisive factor in the outcome of the case, since it provided the basis for attempted kidnapping charges that Florida prosecutors brought against Nowak, the most serious count she faced. Shipman told police she'd been sprayed in the face, though Nowak's lawyer later uncovered signed statements by paramedics on the scene contradicting Shipman's account (the spray had missed her face, she told them at the time), statements the prosecutors somehow failed to turn over to the defense.

right away as the woman who'd pepper-sprayed her, even though Lisa had changed out of the tan trench coat she'd been wearing into a darker one and her hair was different. Colleen, who thought of herself as having a big nose and was thus inclined to notice other people's noses, had formed a distinct impression of Lisa's while they were sitting on the shuttle bus, and it was the same nose. At this point, she still had no idea who Lisa was. Later, at the airport police station, when the cops asked her if she knew the name Lisa Nowak, she remembered that Bill's ex's name was Lisa but had to call him to find out if her last name was Nowak. She recalled once having seen a picture of Lisa on a poster at the NASA gym during one of her workout sessions with Bill, but she hadn't connected it with the crazy lady in the parking lot. At first, after Bill confirmed Lisa's identity, Colleen thought maybe someone had stolen Lisa's ID and was claiming to be an astronaut, because why would an astronaut want to steal her car?

Of Course That Hurt

When Detective Becton asked Lisa, "Did he break your heart?"—meaning Bill—Lisa answered tearfully, "My husband is the only person who broke my heart." Reading through the rambling, frequently incomprehensible transcript of her interrogation is like being confronted with obscure modernist poetry at its most incoherent, though you do get a distinct picture of what her internal state must have been like: an electrical storm of self-delusion crashing over a roiling ocean of romantic injury. There should have been a small-craft advisory for anyone in the vicinity.

At the outset of the interview, a disjointed Lisa tells Detective Becton that she and the man in question had "more than a working relationship but less than a romantic relationship." She was trying to do damage control ("I don't want to bring other people into it, if it's not necessary"), so refuses to use Bill's name and hedges around about whether they were lovers, implying that they couldn't be since she was still legally married and not really "free" in that respect. Becton plays along, suggesting that they just refer to Bill as "Tim" if Lisa doesn't want to reveal his name—Becton knew it already anyway, from Colleen—letting her know in the usual cop show fashion that if she cooperates he can go to bat for her with his superiors. He defers to her intelligence ("I can tell that you're a very educated woman"), reads to her admiringly from her résumé, which he'd managed to obtain in the hours following the arrest ("You have a bachelor's in science, an aerospace engineering in the Naval Academy [*sic*], a master's of science in aeronautical engineering, and a degree in aeronautical and astronomical energy and engineering from the U.S. Naval postgraduate school"), and cajoles her with sympathy: "For you to be here something serious had to happen to you. . . . Something had to happen for tonight to go down. And if you need help, you know, . . . let's face it, everybody needs help at some point in their life and you can't always do everything by yourself." He's a regular station house Dr. Phil. "You have a lot going on inside of you. It's either a lot of pain, a lot of anger, or it's both. And right now you're bottling it up a lot."

As Lisa discloses more details about the relationship, Becton presses the consoling idea that Bill had been sending mixed signals—it's always pathetically consoling to women when a man calls out another man for romantic bad behavior. Lisa gratefully concurs: Bill had picked her up from the airport two weeks before, and you don't do that for just anybody! Becton commiserates: "He's showing you that it's more than just friendship. But then he's telling you that it's just friendship, and actions speak louder than words." They're like two girlfriends decoding puzzling male behavior over margaritas. "You need to dump him out of your head," Becton advises. "Girl, you're just startin' over!"

Becton has a less chummy agenda, of course; he wants Lisa to tell him where her car is parked so he won't have to search every airport lot for it. Lisa, for her part, wants Becton to tell her what Colleen has said about her relationship with Bill ("Can you tell me what she talked to you about? That would help," she wheedles), correctly surmising that if Becton's heard about her from Colleen, then Colleen does indeed know about Bill's relationship with her—knowledge that seems desperately important to Lisa. Evidently something in her makeup—pride? grief?—had prevented her from just asking Bill directly and sparing herself a lot of travail:

NOWAK: Did you tell her who I was?

BECTON: Yes, I mentioned your name. She says she's never met you.

NOWAK: But she knows me?

BECTON: She knew of you.

NOWAK: Okay.

Becton testified at a pretrial hearing that the interview with Nowak was the hardest of his entire career. It was like a chess game and he felt overmatched: "I realized I was dealing with somebody who was more intelligent than I was—more educated." This seems unduly modest given how masterfully he manipulated her, so much so that her statements to the police were later thrown out by the judge, who ruled her revelations were coerced. There's no doubt that Nowak was a smart cookie—all those degrees!—and used to getting by on brainpower. Astronauts are technocrats, after all: if anyone knows that information is power it's someone who's been shot into orbit and kept there by virtue of astrodynamic calculations. Dazed and sleep-deprived, holding on to her fraying rationality by a thread, Lisa was still bent on using what info she had as a bargaining chip to find out what Colleen knew—she keeps promising Becton she'll tell him where the car is *later*. (He accuses her angrily of thinking he has "stupid" written on his forehead.) But at another level she was clueless: she keeps asking to speak to Shipman—she seems to think if she can just talk to Colleen and *explain,* she can get her to drop the charges. Becton tells her that's not going to happen. At that point Lisa is still clinging to the delusion that NASA might not have to be notified (she even wonders if she might be able to get back to work the next day), and Becton strings her along, telling her he hasn't contacted NASA security yet. "I can step up to the plate and speak up for you," he promises—*if* she tells him what he wants to know. Eventually he breaks it to her that the FBI has to be informed since the assault took place on federal property and involved federal employees, around which time reality starts sinking in, like a sledgehammer to the head.

Nowak's motive for the stalking, according to the press, was that she "wanted to know where she stood in the love triangle." But this isn't entirely accurate: Lisa knew where she stood—she'd been jettisoned for another woman. What she wanted was for Colleen to know where *she* stood. If you follow her logic, which I admit to finding not entirely alien, the issue she'd fastened onto was timing. Bill and Colleen had met at the end of November. Bill told Lisa about the relationship at the beginning of January. It was now the beginning of February. When Lisa keeps telling Becton that Colleen doesn't have all the "information," what she's apparently trying to say is that there was a period of *overlap*, during which neither of them knew about the other. In her words: "Of course there is a period of time when you find out you didn't know what was going on, and of course that hurt."

Of course that hurt. What a lot of personal carnage condensed into four little words. And was Colleen aware of this overlap too, or happily oblivious to the existence of this minor complication, this other interested party? This was Lisa's question, and depending on the answer she would perhaps be in a position to convey a hurtful truth to the pretty young Colleen, who, according to her statement, did indeed think she and Bill had been exclusive for the previous two months. What exactly did Lisa want Colleen to know—that Bill wasn't such a hero after all? Or was it that the affair with Lisa had continued even into January, even after Bill had said it was over? Such things have been known to happen—you work out together or go for a bike ride, someone showers at someone else's place . . . "I mean, why only be honest with me, why not be honest with her also?" Lisa demands of Becton, her state-appointed confessor, about what she suspects has been Bill's policy of selective truth telling. It was the galling inequality of it that allowed her to convince herself that confronting Colleen was in Colleen's best interests. "If some people don't know, then that's not the right kind of situation. . . . I very much wanted to set it right."

If the road to scandal is sometimes paved with good intentions, the desire to think the best of your own intentions is another snare in the already problematic business of self-examination. Social psychologists have a name for it: "the holier-than-thou effect"—a self-inflating bias when it comes to assessing one's own motives and sincerity. In Lisa's case, the obsession with rectifying the information imbalance between her and Colleen soon overtook all self-protection and rationality, swaddling the festering romantic wound with a purpose— enough of one to propel her those 950 long, solitary miles to

Orlando. She didn't want to *hurt* Colleen, she insisted. She just thought that if Colleen had *all the information* . . . Then what? Would something have been altered? Was Nowak really thinking that some sort of enlightened three-way arrangement might get negotiated, if everything were out in the open? That's what she seems to imply when she tells Becton that if everyone knows about what's going on and "they're all okay with it, you don't have to make a choice if everyone's okay." Becton asks incredulously, "So if he was going to date both of you that would be acceptable to you?" Lisa says that it depends. This is too much for Becton, clearly more of a traditionalist about such things: "How can you tell me you'd be okay with this guy being with the both of you at the same time!"

Apparently Lisa *was* willing to share Bill, at least until her divorce came through ("I had no intention of forcing choices," she tells Becton)—but first she had to find out what Colleen knew and when she knew it. How Lisa thought she'd elicit the relevant details at 4 a.m., dressed in her absurd garage-sale disguise, having first doused Colleen with pepper spray or incapacitated her with some other tool from her henchman's arsenal—this she hadn't entirely worked out. The road trip itself had the same dreamy logic: it was supposed to repair something, it was meant to assuage an injury. Lisa did tell Becton that she hadn't decided in advance whether to clue in Colleen that Bill had misled them both. But why not spread the hurt around?

It was Becton who nailed it on the head: Lisa was obviously a lot angrier at Bill than either she or he cared to know.

Whether or not Bill had been romantically confusing—and it wouldn't exactly be a first in human history—Lisa, despite her placid exterior, had clearly forgiven him exactly nothing. Some part of her had to be aware that at the end of the day Bill would be exposed along with her, that they'd end up in the toilet together. Aside from their image-dependent public roles, they were both active military, and the military still has a funny way of court-martialing people for adultery. Sure enough, the toilet was just where Billy O. landed—a public laughingstock, the flyboy-lothario, his career in shreds along with hers. If I were Lisa, or anyone else who'd ever been abruptly jilted in a self-serving, mealymouthed way (especially for someone younger!), in some feral corner of my being I might not have been entirely displeased with this turn of events.

And why *should* she have forgiven him, by the way? Here we come to the heart of this scandal: forgiveness is the least innate of impulses. Or as psychoanalyst Theodor Reik, one of Freud's inner circle, puts it in a bracing little essay on forgiveness and vengeance: "Only fools, hypocrites or sick people deny the deep and voluptuous satisfaction adequate revenge can give, deny the extraordinary feeling of liberation, indeed redemption from stifling psychic pressure, which follows successful revenge." Reik scoffs at the idea that there's anything "natural" about forgiving someone who's hurt you, dismissing it as empty sentimentality. "On the contrary, it is a very unnatural reaction," he insists. "Nothing could be more plausible and natural for people than to take revenge." Forgiveness is a far weaker impulse than retaliation, which is, perversely, only strengthened by all the guilty attempts to repress it. And the fewer outlets modern culture makes available for vengeance—no more duels or honor killings, unfortunately—the more intense the repressed tendencies become. Forgiveness simply doesn't exist in the unconscious, says Reik. There's little emotional significance in these socially imposed acts of conciliation that we're all supposed to perform for propriety's sake, no matter how self-congratulatory they make you feel—the conciliation ritual is undoubtedly one of the biggest shams around.

The problem for society is that the desire for revenge is so intense it has to be sublimated into more socially acceptable forms. That's the true origin of forgiveness, says Reik—it's not noble to forgive, since at an emotional level forgiving someone is really just a backdoor attempt to humiliate the supposed object of your largesse: payback in another guise, gussied up as righteousness. Anyone who's ever felt the warm bath of smugness that accompanies being the "better person" in such situations probably knows what he means, or might if self-transparency were remotely possible. "Yes, one must forgive one's enemies," Reik quotes Heinrich Heine approvingly, "but not until they are hanged." Trundling from Houston to Orlando in her silver Saturn on her spurned lover's mission, Lisa was a perfect object lesson in the emptiness of turning the other cheek.

Women Drivers

Clearly scandal favors certain motifs, but is it also drawn to particular locales? The question arises because, oddly enough, another spectacular revenge scandal had erupted just a few years before in the same bedroom community south of Houston where Nowak and her husband lived, involving yet another scorned woman behind the wheel. This was Clara Harris, a forty-five-year-old dentist who claimed that running over her unfaithful ortho-dontist-husband, David, with her Mer-cedes in the parking lot of the hotel she'd discovered him at in the company of their receptionist (the Harrises shared a dental practice in addition to a can-cerous marriage) was an accident. David died of his injuries, which included a broken back, pelvis, jaw, and multiple smashed ribs.

Initially, after David confessed the three-month affair, Clara did try forgiveness (first firing the receptionist), though as Reik might have predicted, it didn't take. The night David broke the news, he and Clara went to a bar together to talk over the situation. Though David promised to end the affair, he also justified his straying by telling Clara that she was overweight, pessimistic, and a workaholic and that she domi-nated conversations, whereas Gail, the receptionist/love-object, a thirty-nine-year-old former beauty queen, was, by contrast, petite, an optimist, and the perfect fit to sleep with; in fact he could sleep all night holding her. This last bit of information was particularly devastating to Clara, since David had never slept holding *her* all night, though on the plus side, Clara did have prettier hands, feet, and eyes. (Clara kept notes about the conversation on a cocktail napkin that was later introduced into evidence at her trial.)

Though David sounds like a husband anyone would be well rid of, apparently he had his charms, since within a day Clara embarked on a whirlwind plan to save their ten-year marriage by becoming everything she thought David wanted in a wife. This included quitting her job, having sex with him three times a night (or so she testified), cooking his favorite meals, hiring a personal trainer, and beginning bronzing sessions at a tanning salon. Her checkbook, which police found in the dented Mercedes following the homicide, was a manic itemized record of female abjection, with carbons for checks written in the days leading up to David's death to a hair salon (she'd decided to go blond), a spa, a nail salon, a lingerie shop, a clothing store, a gym ($1,277.35 for a one-year membership), and two checks to a plastic surgeon with whom she'd scheduled both liposuction and breast enlargement surgery. There was also a check made out to the private detective agency she hired to trail David (which was how she learned he was at the hotel), the rather whimsically named Blue Moon Investigations, one of whose employees, stationed in the hotel parking lot with a video camera, ended up being perfectly situated to film their client plowing down her husband with her car.

And one final check, to a local Baptist church for its building fund: if the plastic surgery god didn't come through, maybe the other one would.

The hotel, the Nassau Bay Hilton, happened to be the same one where the Harrises had gotten married ten years earlier on Valentine's Day. (It also happened to be across the road from the Johnson Space Center, where Lisa Nowak worked.) Now, just a week after David's confession to Clara and following a romantic late-afternoon lunch at a lake-view table, he and Gail had checked into a room. Did he really *have* to go to the same hotel—does Houston have only one of them? Not only had David promised to break off the affair, he'd even confessed it to his parents and daughter; the purpose of the lunch was supposedly to end things with Gail, and Clara had agreed to a final meeting. Learning that David was at a hotel instead, Clara instructed the nanny to pack a week's worth of clothes in an old suitcase and throw the rest of his wardrobe in the trash. Arriving at the Hilton in lethal form, she demanded the desk clerk call David's room, but there was no record of him; he'd checked in under an assumed name. Clara finally reached him on his cell, inventing an emergency at home; when David and Gail appeared in the lobby Clara sprang on Gail, tearing her blouse. Hotel security guards broke up the fight, and the ménage retreated to the parking lot, where Clara keyed her former receptionist's Lincoln Navigator, leaving deep scratches along the sides and rear, then ripped off the windshield wiper blades as her coup de grâce.

David was heading for his own car when Clara careened into him with her Mercedes. There would later be disagreement between the defense and state pathologists about exactly how many times he'd been run over, though it appeared to have been more than once. David may have been king of the cads, but Clara managed to lose whatever wronged-female sympathy vote she might have accrued by virtue of having David's seventeen-year-old daughter with her in the car, as if to punish the child for the crimes of the father, in the classical mode. (Euripides' Medea springs to mind, the original spurned woman—"Her mood is dangerous, nor will she brook her cruel treatment," another character remarks of her—though Medea killed her children rather than her philandering husband, a somewhat more wrenching denouement.) Lindsey Harris testified against her stepmother at the trial, tearfully disputing Clara's testimony that it had been an accident. "She stepped on the accelerator and went straight for him," she told the jurors. "She said, 'I'm so sorry, I'm so sorry, it was an accident.' She knew what she did and she wasn't sorry." Clara sobbed throughout her trial, shaking and weeping so loudly during the coroner's testimony about her husband's injuries— some fifty autopsy photos of David Harris's body were shown to the jury—that the (female) judge warned, "We're just not going to have a big show going on." The jury concurred that Clara's crime was "an act of sudden passion" as her lawyer had argued—a peculiarly Texan legal throwback to the code of the Old West—but sentenced her to twenty years anyway. At the sentencing hearing her pastor argued for probation in lieu of prison, noting that under biblical law David and Gail had committed the sin of adultery. He didn't prevail, but at least that building fund check Clara wrote didn't go entirely to waste.*

Reports occasionally surface of an obscure human tribe that lacks the propensity to overvalue those who've abandoned them, but reports occasionally surface of unicorn sightings too. The rest of us are left muddling through with makeshift forms of revenge that, in deference to social proprieties, usually stop short of outright slaughter. Sharklike divorce lawyers and murderous property settlements generally have to do, though how can even the worst financial punishments suffice when someone's fallen out of love with you? You want them *dead*. Clara Harris's murderous impulse isn't hard to fathom; what's less clear is why she not only mowed down her husband in front of as many witnesses as she could assemble on short notice but also arranged to have the act captured on videotape, as though preparing the evidence for her own prosecution. Perhaps the score settling wasn't with David alone: Clara blamed herself for the affair (if only she'd been thinner), then punished her husband for succumbing, then punished herself for administering the punishment. Clara Harris may have

---

*The inevitable made-for-TV movie, *Suburban Madness*, came two years later. The television treatment of women murdering their husbands tends to be sympathetic these days (playing to the secret fantasies of the genre's core demographic?), melodrama veering toward kitsch; the screenplays take an arch and knowing tone toward the male victims and their treacheries, and the actresses playing the leads invariably push it up a couple of notches, like late-period Joan Crawford.

killed her husband, but it's not as though she wasn't also deeply beholden to social proprieties; unfortunately, they're not so easy to elude.

Justice for All

Angry women with driver's licenses: let's assume we haven't heard the last from this constituency when it comes to future scandals, to be filed under American crack-ups generally, or attachment disorders in our time.* Clara Harris's checkbook should be on permanent exhibit at the Smithsonian in the wing devoted to artifacts of American family life. So should an equally agonized item found in Lisa Nowak's car: a hand-written letter to Bill Oefelein's mother thanking her for her encouraging notes about Lisa and Bill's relationship. "Bill is absolutely the best person I've ever known and I love him more than I knew possible. Your kindness of supporting us, even under such circumstances as have existed in the past is nothing short of extraordinary," Lisa had written in a neat girlish hand. She's referring to her own marital situation, which, she reports, is "finally coming to a close with the for-mal separation and separate living arrangements accom-plished"; she's now in the process of completing the official divorce paperwork. Her own parents hadn't been nearly as

---

*A woman who thinks she loves a man she deeply hates is not an unfamiliar phe-nomenon, as Diana Trilling remarked of a previous Mrs. Harris (Jean), who killed her lover, diet doctor guru Herman Tarnower, a few decades ago.

supportive, she confides, and it means a lot to her to have another mom to turn to. "It has been my privilege and honor to receive such special caring from you," she effuses. Who knows whether this letter was meant to be mailed, or what Lisa's relationship actually was with Bill's mother; Lisa was, after all, in something of a delusional state. But she did tell Becton that she'd met Bill's kids for the first time the previous month at his apartment—apparently she'd met his whole family. In the semiotics of relationships such events have been known to be taken as signs though, needless to say, such signs can be misleading and open to multiple interpretations, which can be crazy-making in itself.

The notable element in both these scorned-women-in-cars scandals is their economy, the way they manage to accomplish two opposite purposes simultaneously: first the infraction, then the punishment for it, neatly tied up with a bow. According to Reik, vengeance directed outward has a tendency to boomerang and be redirected inward, transformed into self-inflicted punishment for an unacceptable aggressive impulse. Not in every case, obviously: people get away with all sorts of things that we never hear about, that don't make the front pages and don't wreck their lives. It would certainly be useful to know what distinguishes those who get caught from those who get a free ride—at least it's the question every prospective vengeance-seeker will want answered. Reading Reik between the lines for tips on extracting revenge, I believe his implication is that *virtuous types* are the group most likely to set themselves up for social punishment. Here's a gloomy thought: the ruthless let themselves off the hook for their aggressions, while those with overactive superegos string themselves up on home-made scaffolds.

Whatever injuries their boyfriends and husbands dealt Nowak and Harris in the romantic realm, their self-inflicted injuries were a thousand times more devastating. You'd think that soliciting national ridicule and turning yourself into an emotional sideshow—not to mention twenty or so years in the slammer—would vastly outweigh the pain of a lover's rejection. It's like chopping off your hand to get over a head-ache, though people in acute pain sometimes attempt desper-ate remedies.

"Do you feel better?" Becton asked Lisa, winding up the interrogation, as if he hadn't just spent five hours getting her to incriminate herself. Lisa says that she does, then wonders—still in the grip of her idée fixe despite the lengthy catharsis—if she can possibly see Colleen. Reading this, you don't know whether to scream at her or laugh, or just concede the fact that loss can have a way of deranging a person's reality checks. However unbalanced her nighttime exploit may have been, it's not so difficult to identify with the hope that trying hard enough will fix things, that carrying out some risk-it-all ordeal, making the dramatic gesture—crashing the wedding, kidnap-ping the beloved, incapacitating the rival—*will* make some-one care again and give you back what you've lost, though it usually works out better in the movies.

In Nowak's case, the attempted murder charges were even-tually dropped, though the attempted kidnapping and battery charges stood; the Florida prosecutors were determined to milk the case for every shred of publicity. Nowak pled not guilty, was released on $25,500 bail, and eventually entered a temporary insanity plea. After a series of rather masterful legal maneuvers by her attorney, Don Lykkebak, who dismantled the state's case piece by piece by getting much of the relevant evidence excluded, Nowak pleaded guilty to felony burglary and misdemeanor battery and was sentenced to a year of probation. (She could have faced up to life in prison if the attempted kidnapping charge had stood.) In the months following the arrest, Nowak and Oefelein were both dropped from the astronaut corps—a first in NASA history—and reassigned to their military positions. But you can see NASA's dilemma: as we learned from Tom Wolfe in *The Right Stuff,* astronauts are NASA's funding chips, kept around to personify the space mission when congressional appropriations are being handed out; if NASA hadn't needed space heroes for public relations purposes, they'd have sent monkeys up there. The fact is that astronauts spend far less time in space than they do cutting rib-

bons at shopping malls and delivering high school commencement addresses: as sullied heroes, the tabloid caption "Lust in Space" trailing after them in perpetuity, Nowak and Oefelein wouldn't exactly do for such occasions.

Colleen Shipman made her first public appearance at a deposition in June. Blond and petite, with a pointy, resolute chin (and not so large-nosed, despite her fears), she clutched the muscular Oefelein firmly by the arm, her trophy.* She looked good. A few months later, when Nowak's lawyer petitioned to remove the GPS ankle monitoring bracelet she had to wear as a condition of bail, Shipman made another court appearance to voice her objections. "Absolutely not," she protested, when asked by the prosecutor if Nowak should be allowed to remove the device. She'd been the victim of an assault, she said, and felt much safer knowing that Nowak was wearing the bracelet. Shipman also strongly objected to Nowak's eventual plea deal, telling the judge that she believed she'd escaped a horrible death that night and that she still suffered from nightmares, migraines, and high blood pressure. Every stranger she saw was a potential attacker. She'd bought a shotgun and obtained a concealed weapon permit.

No forgiveness for *her*. It seemed like she was enjoying her moment in the spotlight.

When someone you love dumps you for someone new, puts pictures of her on his desk in the office you share (was this *really* necessary?), and lets everyone at work know he's got a new sweetie, the premise is that you suffer a bit, then move

---

*Shipman and Oefelein both left the military shortly later and moved to his home state of Alaska, where they eventually got engaged. They've also started a business promoting themselves as adventure writers and motivational speakers.

on. You get over your pain in private instead of acting it out on the national stage for the mass entertainment of your fellow citizens. Nowak's feelings were just too incontinent: she was the quintessential leaky vessel. The spectacle of a personality so flamboyantly turned against itself, meticulously organizing such lavish public humiliations right down to those diapers, the possibility that any of us might be driven to such lengths by an unexpected blow to the ego, was just too grotesque. No wonder we were laughing so hard.

CHAPTER 2

AN UNREASONABLE JUDGE

Calamity

The temptation to judge those who fall out of line *is* irresistible, all the more when the line-crossing involves what we like to refer to as hubris, for instance when someone who's chosen judgment as a profession, issuing verdicts on other people's slip-ups, flagrantly flouts the law himself. This is unreasonable behavior, and since the concept of the "reasonable person" is at the foundation of our legal system and thus underpins organized social life as we know it, it's tantamount to sabo-

tage from within.* Reasonableness is supposed to be personi-
fied in the figure of the black-robed judge, thus garbed
because only the head matters, reason's locale. He sits physically raised above the rest of us, and we're commanded to rise
in his presence (or hers) to demonstrate our deference, both to
the individual judge and to the law itself. After all, where
would we be without them—in chaos or some brute state of
nature, clawing and killing with impunity, driving through
red lights, heisting one another's property.

Enter Sol Wachtler, once the chief justice of the New
York State Court of Appeals (New York's highest court),
and a *very* unreasonable man. Here was monumental irrationality enacted from within reason's highest chambers,
into which scandal crept, spotted its quarry, and sprung like
a viper. One of the most riveting aspects of this story—aside
from the full-throttle plummet into
professional ruin, national humiliation, and hellish imprisonment—was
its narrative symmetry, as the eventual
comeuppance was meted out by the
very system that had elevated Wachtler
to the lofty pinnacles from which he
engineered his subsequent plunge: the
law. It had a certain elegance.

---

*Reasonableness is the leitmotif of the American courtroom ("reasonable doubts,"
"reasonable expectations," "reasonable expenses"), even though it's basically a
necessary fiction: it imagines we're characters divorced from passion, imagination, and irrationality, which is generally less than evident.

This is also a tale of compartmentalization in its finest hour. Wachtler's plunge was so rife with nose-thumbing theatrics that he seemed, perversely, to be soliciting punishment. (Most of us try to avoid it.) It must be said that the compartmentalization wasn't Wachtler's alone, since the methods by which the law chooses to punish those felled by unreason are, ironically, among the most perverse aspects of the judicial system, even in these enlightened times. It's not hard to see why: unreason marks the limits of the social order, and those of us who rely on the social order—i.e., everyone—don't like being reminded of its inherent flimsiness.

It was a Saturday afternoon in November 1992 when the chief judge, who was on his way to buy bagels, was pulled over on the Long Island Expressway by six FBI agents in three different vehicles, thrown up against the fender, cuffed, and read his rights. "What did I do?" pleaded Wachtler, terrified. He was being charged with extortion, they told him. More charges would follow, a whole laundry list of them. Wachtler was, at the time, one of the country's foremost legal figures, even mentioned occasionally as a potential Supreme Court nominee (and by a few hopeful liberal Jews as the first Jewish president one day, a Jewish Kennedy, they liked to say), though as an anti–death penalty, pro-choice, pro-labor Republican, he obviously wasn't ever going to be nominated by a Republican president. He was, however, the anointed Republican candidate for the upcoming 1994 New York gubernatorial race against the incumbent, Democrat Mario Cuomo, a former pal of his (more about this curious friendship to come), and on the verge of announcing his candidacy. His wife, Joan, though not entirely thrilled about his decision to run, had been at Saks shopping for campaign outfits that very morning. It was all over the news in a matter of hours; judges and politicians across the state were being called away from their golf games, pagers were vibrating. Was it some kind of a bad joke? *Sol Wachtler?*

The scandal annals are packed with examples of those who've turned the codes and venues of professional life into opportunities for creative self-sabotage: journalists invent stories (as if no one's going to notice), CEOs cook the books (have they never heard of audits?), people get themselves into all sorts of pickles. Still, when Sol Wachtler was arrested everyone's first reaction was that it had to be a mistake. He'd always been scandal-free and incorruptible and, despite having come up through the often seamy ranks of New York State party politics (a protégé of Nelson Rockefeller's), regarded as a paragon of virtue. And what a legal reputation! Known as an innovative and progressive thinker, he'd authored a stream of groundbreaking precedents throughout his tenure on the Court of Appeals on the most important issues of the day—free speech, minority rights, obscenity, even decisions opposing mandatory drug testing—all of which he'd penned, as he later would his extortion notes, from the desk of his legal hero, legendary former New York chief judge and U.S. Supreme Court justice Benjamin Cardozo.

In short, Sol Wachtler seemed like the last person on earth who'd invent an alter ego named David Purdy, a fat down-on-his-luck private detective from Houston, and, while impersonating Purdy, threaten his former girlfriend, Joy Silverman (a socialite who happened to have access to the private phone number of the head of the FBI), with the various harms that would befall her if she didn't hand over a lot of money for dirty photos he claimed he had of her. There were no photos, just an unleashed imagination and, soon to follow, the consequences of letting it loose in public. For the record, an imagination in full throttle is about as socially welcome as raw sewage sluicing into the living room, which was roughly how Judge Wachtler came to be seen.

In his more constrained moments, Sol Wachtler had cut a charismatic figure, though he sometimes struck people as a little too steeped in his own rectitude, even a bit asexual. Still boyishly handsome at sixty-two, if anxious about it (he'd had a face-lift recently and, in his younger days, a nose job), he'd been known as a trim and snappy dresser, even appearing on the occasional best-dressed list, once alongside another noted character actor, Laurence Olivier. He was a sought-after speaker, admired for his charm and wit—he definitely knew how to work a crowd, with just the right combination of erudition and self-deprecating humor. Married for forty years, with four children, he played the indulgent dad (Joan's role was disciplinarian), but the marriage, as sometimes happens, had become stale and sexless: Sol was never there, and when he was, he was preoccupied. Joan, aggrieved that things had changed between them, turned away, first going back to school to get a degree, then immersing herself in a new career as a social worker.

Sol, no lothario and even a bit of a prude—he hated dirty jokes and made it known that he didn't tolerate obscenity—had guiltily succumbed to a secret affair with his wife's stepcousin Joy, even though he'd always been strenuously against adultery. "I was one of the first to criticize a person, male or female, who strayed into those forbidden pastures," he'd later say. But how could he resist? Joy had practically made a campaign out of seducing him, first asking around to see whether he had affairs, then showing up uninvited at his speeches and gushing to him afterward about how fantastic he was. She sent expensive gifts to the house and called him constantly for advice or on whatever pretense she could find. When the straitlaced Sol still didn't take the hint, she drove though a blinding snowstorm to surprise him at a speech in Albany, then cornered him in his office afterward, demanding to be kissed. Or so Wachtler said; Joy claimed that it was Sol who'd pursued *her* (though her own friends disputed her version). Whoever initiated things, to a covertly vain man in a celibate marriage who'd never fooled around, this had to be pretty heady stuff—"an excursion of breathless exhilaration," to use Sol's words (he proved to have a rather ornate prose style, particularly on this subject). After a few weeks of demurrals on his part, the two embarked on a passionate romance, sometimes talking seven or eight times a day on the phone while Wachtler's law clerks waved briefs at him, trying fruitlessly to get his attention.

Joy was seventeen years younger, dark-haired, dramatically attractive, and very rich; at that point she was on her third marriage. She had a bad temper, an insecure streak, a Park Avenue

apartment, an astrologer, a psychic, a psychotherapist, and a bichon frise named after Coco Chanel. The current husband was a wealthy businessman, though Joy also had her own money, inherited from her stepfather, a real estate magnate. Sol Wachtler was an executor of the trust, which was how the future lovers had gotten to know each other.

The aptly named Joy reintroduced Sol to sex, and he, in return, offered her the chance to become a woman of substance. Under his tutelage, like a Park Avenue Eliza Doolittle, Joy began fashioning a new identity for herself, blossoming from a lady-who-lunches into a major player in Republican fund-raising efforts for the first George Bush's presidential campaign. It turned out she had a talent for it (having a lot of rich friends and a rich husband helped), and Sol mentored her in the art of political schmooze, from drafting her thank-you notes to telling her which bigwigs to cultivate at social events. Local Bush staffers didn't quite know what to make of Joy, who overdressed and turned up at the campaign office to stuff envelopes accompanied by her chauffeur and limo. But party higher-ups were impressed, and Joy's labors were rewarded, as things are in these echelons, when Bush Senior, now in the White House, nominated her for an ambassadorship to Barbados. Wachtler had advised asking for Luxembourg, then settling for something in the Caribbean, which was just what she did. Unfortunately, Joy, who had never held a job and lacked a college degree, was soon pegged by a *Washington Post* op-ed as a "major exhibit" in a flap about wealthy fund-raisers buying ambassadorships and became the target of even more acid commentary when word got out that prior to her confirmation she'd already flown to Barbados to inspect the official residence; her then husband, finding the place too small, arranged to rent a second residence next door. Sol tirelessly coached Joy for the confirmation hearing, but in the end the appointment fell through and someone else got Barbados. Silverman remained a pal of both Bushes nevertheless, supping at the White House (she also dined with V.P. Dan Quayle at his residence) and weekending at Camp David. George Bush, said to be rather entranced with the lustrous Joy, eventually named her to the board of trustees of the Kennedy Center, which luckily didn't require Senate confirmation.

Soon after the flirtation with politics ended, Joy divorced her husband after hiring a private detective to trail him and telling friends she had proof he'd been having an affair (he denied it), though neglecting to mention her own multi-year affair with Sol. Now single and understandably antsy about her future, needy and excitable to begin with, Joy began pushing Sol to leave Joan and generally making life hellish. Her demands were many: for expensive jewelry (she suggested Van Cleef & Arpels), for constant reassurances and declarations of his love in front of friends. Pressured, guilt-plagued, and in desperate need of relief after four and a half years of vacillating between wife and girlfriend—even seeing Joy's psychotherapist to help him ease out of the marriage and at one point telling Joan he wanted a trial separation—Sol finally ended the affair. (Yes, he broke up with *her*, another baffling aspect of this tale.)

I'm a Sick and Desperate Man

People end affairs every day—it was the way Wachtler went about it that may furrow a few brows. He appears to have been a man with a talent for less than direct ways of negotiating life's difficult moments; perhaps a harbinger of trouble to come, though in the aftermath of a scandal, every quirk can look like a harbinger. His exit strategy was to tell Joy he had an inoperable brain tumor; he was just back from the Mayo Clinic and his motor skills were already going. There's some possibility that Wachtler himself semi-believed this story: he had a tendency toward hypochondria, combined with an aversion to doctors, and there were assorted ailments he refused to consult anyone about; he also refused to have an MRI, because he was claustrophobic, so had self-diagnosed his condition with the help of medical textbooks. Joy consulted her astrologer, who confirmed that Sol did indeed have a brain tumor. Loyally Joy swore to stick by him, and they continued seeing each other sporadically, even sleeping together on occasion, though Sol encouraged her to date. Sol also continued seeing Joy's psychotherapist, who practiced in Philadelphia and seems to have been one of the more boundary-challenged members of the profession, taking four or five phone calls a day from Joy and letting Joy and Sol use her house for week-end assignations. Whatever psychotherapy was being conducted didn't seem to help stabilize Wachtler's more erratic leanings.

Despite the ongoing involvement between Sol and Joy, there were obviously hurt feelings on both sides, and Joy was getting fed up with Sol's taking her to obscure restaurants in Queens to avoid running into anyone they knew. She asked friends to fix her up with someone, which was how, nine months later, she met David Samson, a handsome (and available) lawyer who was soon accompanying her to dinners at the White House. At the beginning she concealed the relationship from Sol, but she finally told him she was seeing someone, and when he wouldn't stop pressing her for details, she took to taunting him that Samson was richer and better looking than he was. Or according to Wachtler she did; Joy denies it—who wouldn't?—though her first husband reported getting identical taunts about the man who succeeded him. (It's possible that he, too, had his axes to grind with Joy.) On many of the events to follow, Sol's and Joy's accounts vary, but one thing is certain. Around this time New York's chief judge embarked on the time-honored adolescent breakup ritual: repeated hang-up phone calls that continued for months. Eventually these escalated into a series of lewd and threatening unsigned notes, at which point, like a harried boss hiring additional staff to handle an increased work load, Wachtler invented two alter egos who took over the task of harassing Joy. He'd later say it was all just a device to get Joy to turn to him for help, perhaps to rekindle their affair (the one he himself had ended), though perhaps this doesn't entirely suffice as an explanation. But as we've seen, scandalizers themselves aren't always the best sources for coherent explanations about why things went the way they did or tumbled out of control, which isn't to say they won't soliloquize at length on these matters whenever the chance arises—in TV interviews, at sentencing hearings, and in their now inevitable memoirs.

Detective David Purdy, Wachtler's first alter ego, told Joy he'd been hired to investigate David Samson's business dealings. Wachtler contrived an elaborately colorful history for Purdy, who described himself, in the course of his numerous threatening phone calls to Joy, as a toothless, incontinent diabetic: *"I lost one kidney and I'm losing another. I'm wearing a diaper now,"* Purdy told Joy, speaking into one of those spy store voice-altering devices. *"I've lost my teeth. I weigh over two hundred pounds. I'm a dying man."* (Diapers again! Were Wachtler and Nowak rummaging through the same prop closet?)

Wachtler also made harassing calls, as Purdy, to both David Samson's ex-wife and Joy Silverman's previous husband, though not before he'd researched Purdy thoroughly, throwing himself into his character like a Method actor handed the role of a lifetime. He even called the Houston YMCA to inquire about room rates as part of his preparation; since Purdy was down on his luck at the time, he couldn't afford classier accommodations. To further delve into the persona, Wachtler bought himself a Stetson, a string tie, and cowboy boots and, after wearing this regalia out in public on a few test runs, showed up in full costume at David Samson's apartment. He had a message to deliver to Samson, he informed the doorman. For this performance, Wachtler adopted a Texas drawl, stretching his lips over his teeth to give the impression of toothlessness, since according to Purdy his gums were in such bad shape he couldn't get fitted for false teeth; he also stuffed extra clothes under his shirt and puffed his stomach out to make himself seem fat. He must have looked like an opera bouffe Sam Spade.*

But who had hired Purdy to investigate Samson? Purdy needed a client list, which was how Wachtler came to invent his second alter, Theresa O'Connor, a middle-aged New Jersey housewife and devout Catholic who was working to oppose an incinerator project Samson was involved with. It was O'Connor who'd hired Purdy to look into Samson's business affairs, Purdy divulged. Once again, Wachtler threw himself into his preparations with the zeal of a theater major. To familiarize himself with the fictional Theresa's milieu, he drove to the town of Linden, New Jersey, where he envisioned she lived; he visited a church where he imagined she prayed; he even talked to the church's priest over the phone to ask

---

*Also oddly reminiscent of the drawling, sweating, potbellied, Stetson-wearing private detective played by veteran character actor M. Emmet Walsh in the Coen brothers' 1984 Texas-noir *Blood Simple*. Both detectives trafficked in faked photos, though in Wachtler's case faked meant imaginary. In *Blood Simple*, the photos the Walsh character tries to hustle are of a sleeping adulterous couple, doctored to look as though the two had been murdered.

about services. He also mailed letters to Joy from what he decided was Teresa's neighborhood and made phone calls impersonating her with his handy voice-altering device. The fact that Theresa was from New Jersey would play a major role in Wachtler's eventual downfall, since mailing the letters from Linden added interstate travel to the indictment, a felony count, as Wachtler would certainly know, even if Theresa didn't. As with Lisa Nowak's to-do list, note the ability to sustain technical rationality in the midst of unreason, to shut off certain regions of consciousness while others are fully functioning. The problem with being an organized scandalizer is that it doesn't help you later in court, where your very organization will likely be used as legal proof of a sound mental state.

Meanwhile, Detective Purdy's harassment of Joy Silverman escalated into threats that he would kidnap Silverman's fourteen-year-old daughter, Jessica. This was a turning point in the legal case against Wachtler: hang-up phone calls are one thing, kidnap threats are something else entirely when it comes to inviting the hammer of the criminal justice system to smash you over the cranium. Ever since the Lindbergh case in 1932, U.S. law enforcement agencies have been especially aggressive when it comes to kidnapping and kidnap threats; sentencing levels for even attempted kidnapping can be harsher than for actual murders, which is one of the reasons kidnapping for ransom is virtually nonexistent in the United States except on TV crime shows. Undeterred by the escalating punishment potential, Purdy also sent lewd and threatening letters to the teenage Jessica (once including a wrapped condom inside a greeting card of a kitten sniffing a flower), though these were intercepted by Joy. The threats culminated in demands that Silverman pay Purdy the sum of $20,000. Initially this was supposed to be payment for imaginary sex photos Purdy said he had of Silverman and Samson; eventually it became a payment to prevent Jessica's kidnapping. *"I'm a sick and desperate man. I need the money and you'll be hearing from me,"* Purdy snarled to Silverman on the phone though his voice-altering device.

Or rather, snarled to the FBI. Some months earlier, Silverman had told her lawyer, who happened to be an old pal of Wachtler's, to tell Sol she knew that he was the one behind the phone threats, and if he didn't stop she'd go to the FBI. Wachtler responded, via the friend, that Silverman was crazy. This was the last straw for Joy, and being who she was, Silverman didn't just call the local police station to complain, she traveled to Washington to meet with William Sessions, then head of the FBI. The New Jersey branch was on the case the next day (because the letters had been mailed from Linden). Clearly this wasn't going be one of those hushed-up high-society embarrassments with miscreants shipped off for pricey rest cures; when they finally arrested him, the FBI had been trailing Wachtler for five weeks and of course tracing all of Silverman's phone calls. Purdy himself had alluded many times to knowing the phone was tapped and not staying on the line too long, yet he'd continued calling regularly, including from Wachtler's own cell phone. Incipient split personalities, take note: amusing company though your alters can be, they may not always have your best interests at heart; in Wachtler's case, they seemed determined to do him in.

Meanwhile, teams of FBI agents had been coaching Joy on how to get Sol to most effectively incriminate himself, feeding her questions to put to him—or rather, to Purdy—about what he planned to do and what would happen to her if she didn't pay, squirreling away every word for the eventual prosecution. No doubt Joy had her own reasons for wanting to capitalize on this bizarre turn of events: Wachtler still controlled her trust fund despite their breakup and discrediting him would put an end to that, at least. There's no evidence that she actually feared Sol or thought he was prone to violence—the day after his arrest a friend of Joy's told the press that Joy herself said she'd only gone to the FBI to get even with Sol. Also she was thinking of writing a book about her ordeal.

In other words, everyone involved had known for quite some time that Wachtler was behind the threats and that they were crazy talk from someone not exactly himself. Nevertheless the FBI postponed arresting him until he'd committed multiple potential felonies, waiting until "criminal threats" escalated into "criminal acts." The most serious offenses occurred well after the FBI was already trailing Wachtler: they gave him plenty of rope, then sat back and watched him hang himself. Afterward, accusations of prosecutorial overkill flew; the accusers even included the next director of the FBI, Louis Freeh, in a rather astounding breach of the usual fraternalism. Nailing Wachtler had become an intermural blood sport for the various law enforcement branches involved, or as the head of the New York FBI office put it jubilantly after the arrest, "We all feel bad about Wachtler, but in spite of that, I feel like Patton after the tank battle: 'God help me, I love it.'"

Why Would He Have Wanted to Hurt Himself?

Wachtler's self-defense—at the trial, to the media, and in his eventual memoir—was that the delusions and bizarre criminal behavior resulted from undiagnosed manic depression. The experts were less certain, differing about both his mental health and his motives: even those on the defense side couldn't agree on whether there was an underlying condition or a "toxic mania" caused by a bad combination of drugs prescribed by different doctors for his insomnia and various other medical complaints. In fact, the drugs Wachtler was taking included Tenuate, known to cause grandiosity and disinhibition, along with Halcion, known to cause delusions.* The prosecution's

---

*Someday someone will write a social history of Halcion's effect on the culture as its delusional properties have fueled a flourishing literary subgenre in addition to the occasional scandal. Besides Wachtler's memoir there's Philip Roth's *Operation Shylock*, published the year after Wachtler's arrest, which opens with an account of the narrator Philip Roth's Halcion-fueled breakdown and subsequent encounter with an antic alter ego also named Philip Roth, leaving both the first Philip Roth and the reader wondering if the second Philip Roth is merely a Halcion-inspired apparition. (Actress Claire Bloom's bitter memoir *Leaving a Doll's House* describes the collapse of her eighteen-year relationship with the real-life Roth following his real-life bout with Halcion.) Interestingly, Wachtler's alter egos and Roth's are both propriety defilers, ids unleashed. Rather less

phalanx of psychiatrists weighed in with their counter-diagnoses. One said Wachtler had a narcissistic personality disorder "marked by feelings of grandiosity, a lack of empathy for others, and a profound sense of entitlement." Another said he was just naïve about women, with a strong need for attention, thus overly vulnerable to rejection, the sort of man who feels injured to the core when turned down by a woman. Yet another accused him of being merely "lovesick," a state in which a spurned lover develops symptoms that may look like depression but don't rise to the level of mental illness. Wachtler himself said that while he didn't want to be exonerated for anything he'd done ("Being bipolar is not and should not be an excuse for criminal conduct") and insisted on taking full responsibility for his actions, they weren't *voluntary* actions, though he did have to testify to being mentally competent as part of his eventual plea agreement. Still, he was deeply offended that after he'd pleaded diminished capacity the trial judge disregarded the mental illness in the sentencing phase—though he also said he'd have done the same thing if he'd been presiding.

If this sounds contradictory, it was. Wachtler displayed the same tendency for self-contradiction at virtually every juncture; the brilliant legal mind didn't extend its reach to his own situation. Some sort of blind spot intervened. One of the

---

comically, William Styron writes of wrestling with suicide after a period of Halcion use in *Darkness Visible: A Memoir of Madness*.

main impediments to self-coherence was that Wachtler was so fixated on holding Joy accountable for the role he thought she'd played in his demise that he ended up blowing away his own defense strategy, without noticing the contradiction, demanding to know why Joy hadn't called him instead of the F.B.I.—that was all she had to do to the harassment.

But if he could have simply stopped had she asked him to, then he *was* in control—where was the diminished capacity? More to the point, a few weeks before his arrest Sol had told his daughter and son-in-law that Joy was being harassed and that he'd gotten word she suspected he was the harasser. But since even this suspicion didn't prompt Joy to contact him, it only increased his feeling of being the injured party. He seems like a man who enjoyed wallowing in injury—bitter that the FBI hadn't arrested him earlier to prevent further incrimination (after all his years on the bench, did he think they were a social service agency?), bitter at Joy for collaborating with them in the first place. He was as much *her* victim as she was his. He told one interviewer: "Joy never knew her father. A psychiatrist told me that she's been taking it out on men ever since. That she destroys men, one by one." It's hard not to wonder about a psychiatrist who hands a self-exonerating patient such a juicy self-exonerating bone to gnaw on—another Wachtler alter perhaps?

For her part, Joy, who had indeed never known her father, wasn't going to give up her claim to victimhood without a fight. Instead she adopted it as a new public identity, going on to become a spokeswoman for the National Victim Center, which mounted plucky protests against Wachtler's post-prison appearance on *Oprah*, calling it an affront to stalking victims everywhere. Joan Wachtler also launched a few choice public words in a *New York Post* interview at her cousin Joy for her role in Sol's breakdown, not to mention her perfidy in bedding Joan's husband. In the end there were so many victims you needed a score card to sort out the competing claims.

Yet even more than he blamed Joy Silverman, Wachtler held one figure responsible for his downfall. This was Michael Chertoff, then the U.S. district attorney for New Jersey, in charge of Wachtler's arrest and prosecution, who exercised a personal vendetta against him, according to Wachtler. And in Chertoff, the son of a rabbi, Wachtler did manage to acquire a tormentor of biblical severity.* Chertoff had indeed held off on arresting Wachtler until what had been minor harassment ballooned into felony proportions, assigning some *eighty* agents to the case: five cars were following the sixty-two-year-old judge at every minute in the days prior to the arrest, with other agents monitoring him from the DA's office, right up

---

*In his subsequent role as secretary of homeland security in the second Bush administration, Chertoff was one of those held responsible for botching the Hurricane Katrina rescue, infamously declaring, "We are extremely pleased with the response that every element of the federal government, all of our federal partners, have made to this terrible tragedy," while dismissing as "rumors" or "someone's anecdotal version" reports of people dying at the New Orleans Superdome. (Chertoff has a talent for showing up in unsavory settings; before this assignment he'd been special counsel to Republicans on the Senate Whitewater Committee investigating the Clintons' finances.)

until Chertoff's *Dragnet*-style command to his squad: "Take him down." It was Chertoff who led a grand jury to indict Wachtler on five felony counts, which could have meant sixteen years in prison and $250,000 in fines. One of the smallish ironies of this case was that Sol Wachtler, a longtime critic of the grand jury system, was famously the origin of the much-quoted line by his college class-mate Tom Wolfe in *Bonfire of the Vanities* to the effect that any prosecutor can get a grand jury to indict a ham sandwich if that's what he's after. This proved all too prescient.

Chertoff's not so charitable view was that Wachtler was cold, calculating, manipulative, and fully rational; he was sadistic to women and motivated by jealousy, not mental illness, and acting out of anger. *Obviously* Wachtler was in control—he'd planned and executed his stratagems while traveling the country giving speeches and running the state judiciary besides! People are responsible for their own behavior, even when inexplicable! Wachtler wasn't "walking around in a bathrobe and screaming like a banshee," Chertoff scoffed to reporters. Unless Wachtler turned out to have some kind of organic problem, unless there was something pressing on the part of his brain that deals with right and wrong, there were going to be criminal charges. Not only did Chertoff argue against bail, he insisted that Wachtler be manacled to his bed when remanded for psychiatric observation, then insisted on house arrest with Wachtler paying for the security guards as a condition of release. Chertoff also refused to consider any plea deal that didn't involve prison, fighting for the longest sentence possible, and no halfway houses either. Chertoff responded to widespread accusations of zealotry by waving the victim banner himself: he was being punished for doing the job he was hired to do!

What a perfect team they made: Chertoff was a prosecutorial zealot, and Wachtler's dedication to public self-injury invited the severest thwacking—the two of them completed each other in some fundamental way. Then, as if things weren't bad enough, like a frustrated masochist goading the sadist to hit even harder, Wachtler dedicated himself to exacerbating his legal jeopardy in every way possible while in the midst of plea negotiations, embarking on a series of miscalculated media interviews that outraged even his sympathizers. The intention (supposedly) was to discuss the burdens of mental illness from the sufferer's standpoint, which might have bolstered the case for leniency. Instead, Wachtler decided to publicly denounce Chertoff, the FBI, and Joy Silverman herself for not having done something to prevent his crimes. A front-page *New York Times* article responded to the media crusade by criticizing Wachtler for "seeking leniency in the court of public opinion by impugning those who brought him down." This was four days before his sentencing hearing.

Wachtler either didn't read the newspapers or felt he'd done insufficient damage to his cause, since just *one* day before the sentencing hearing, he authorized a payment to himself of almost $40,000 in trustee commissions from Joy Silverman's trust fund—inexplicably he was still serving as the executor—covering the same time period he'd been harassing her. (Wachtler had already received some $800,000 in commissions from Silverman's trust over his years on the job and had lately been threatening to cut her monthly checks; no wonder she wanted his head on a plate.) Silverman contested the payout and tried to get Wachtler removed from the executorship; he retaliated by trying to get his daughter, Lauren, installed in his place. After so many years in charge of Joy's money, he seemed to think of it as his private entitlement. Love and money: how much unreason they educe, how much fungibility, and how many scandal opportunities. Step carefully in these maddening precincts!

In the end, Wachtler got off relatively lightly given the pileup of charges, sentenced to fifteen months with two years of supervised release by a puzzled judge who declared herself unable to either comprehend Wachtler's bizarre behavior or decide which of the warring psychiatric experts to believe. But even this wasn't the end of the wreckage; there were wounds yet to be inflicted. Serving out his sentence at Butner Correctional Institution in North Carolina, a psychiatric prison, Wachtler was mysteriously stabbed in the back while resting on his cot. The two inch-deep wounds just above his shoulder blade were probably made by a fork with a tine removed, authorities later surmised. Based on the location and shallowness and since no one else in the area seemed capable of stabbing anyone, the FBI concluded that the wounds were self-inflicted. Eventually they revised their position since no weapon was found in the vicinity, but not before the details were leaked to the press, outraging Wachtler's family and his private psychiatrist, who demanded to know: "Why would he have wanted to hurt himself?"

Why indeed? Had his own psychiatrist somehow overlooked Wachtler's woeful expertise at self-injury? After all, he'd amassed quite a track record by that point. Striking the same oblivious note; Wachtler himself repeats the plaintive question in his memoir: "How could I stab myself in the back?"

The Enemy Within

Presumably the irony was unintentional, but isn't this the question at the heart of every elaborately choreographed public downfall? *How could I do this to myself?* Or to formulate it more broadly: Is there something self-defeating in human nature that seeks out punishment? After all, self-punishing behavior isn't exactly rare, even among those who stop short of criminal deeds. If in doubt, peruse the self-help aisles of your local bookstore, where you'll find titles such as *Stop Stabbing Yourself in the Back: Zapping the Enemy Within*, in which author Judith Briles cautions against a laundry list of common self-sabotaging behaviors, including egomania, paranoia, blame, perfectionism, and what she labels "negative self-talk." There's no mention of the fork-in-the-back trick, but it's hard not to wonder if some inner punster was having a bit of a laugh at the judge's expense. As it happens, Wachtler *was* known as an inveterate punster, given to pranks, impersonations, and little practical jokes, occasionally with an aggressive edge, according to members of his staff—"Sol's little scams," one staffer called them. The threatening notes to Joy and her daughter were also rife with puns and bad jokes, often sent on greeting cards full of double entendres. If "beating yourself up" over something—imagined shortcomings, a guilty conscience—is one of the common pitfalls of having a superego, stabbing yourself in the back just kicks it up a notch or two. Whatever really transpired at Butner, whether or not Wachtler managed to plunge that particular sharp object into his own back, the double meaning was left hanging there, like a gleeful coda to a strange, sad tale—scandal having a nasty chuckle at another schlub's demise.

Or, here's another way to look at it. One strand of psychoanalytic thinking about crime and punishment proposes that guilt exists before the deed, at least unconsciously. In other words, guilt isn't the consequence of a crime, it's the motive. In such cases, committing an actual crime may even come as a relief since it attaches the unconscious feeling of guilt to something real, to something in the present. From this perspective, punishment would actually be a stimulus to crime, not a deterrent, which obviously complicates society's position in dispensing justice.

As counterintuitive as such theories may sound given humankind's much-touted instinct for survival (supposedly governing every aspect of existence from deep within our genes, at least according to the evolutionary psychology crowd), it's hard not to notice that certain people really *are* their own worst enemies, willing participants in elaborate punishment schemes, and bringing far too much creativity to the enterprise: the varieties of artful self-castigation are many. Consider the accident-prone, who suffer from a particularly "skillful kind of awkwardness," as the literature observes. Or those who organize their lives so that misfortunes will occur, endeavors will fail; they're continually persecuted by blows of fate, which are somehow not unexpected. One term for such tendencies is *social masochism*. Unlike in the more quotidian sexual variety, in this version punishment is solicited not from an individual but from society itself, with the social masochist engineering scenarios that evoke social sadism. As we've seen, this isn't so difficult to attain; the rest of us are more than willing to comply. In fact, it works out well for everyone involved, since the distinctive feature of social masochism is that it requires an audience: the punishment must be received in *public*, the shame displayed to the world, with metaphorically bared buttocks on display for a metaphorical strapping. But what's the appeal of this, what's the inner necessity? Simply that some private tribunal has mandated it; that an overdeveloped sense of guilt requires it.

Like judges, social masochists too spend their days in courtrooms—imaginary ones, that is—replaying scenarios of guilt and punishment. Literature has certainly been the beneficiary: consider Kafka, the world's great explicator of tormented inner prisons, or Dostoevsky's cast of punishment-seeking, confession-spouting sufferers. Wachtler may have lacked the literary prowess of such illustrious predecessors, but there was still something darkly inventive about his brand of self-punishment, an antic quality to those alter egos of his with their makeshift costumes and kooky character tics. And what an inspired dramatic arc he constructed for his audience: the famous judge subjected to the community's collective judgment; the guilty lover brought down by his Joy. One of the defense psychiatrists who examined Wachtler saw it similarly. Wachtler, he testified, was convinced that:

> he is an actor on a stage and the world is his audience. He believes that the thoughts, feelings, and behaviors exhibited during the manic episode will be interpreted in this light—viewed as an astonishing performance, to be appreciated for its inventiveness, its cleverness, but not to be taken seriously or acted upon.

The best scandals often do have this flamboyant quality; they're command performances, which is one reason they demand our attention. There we sit, front row center to someone's self-propelled demolition job, puzzling over the unknowabilities, secretly relishing the painful denouements: exposure, humiliation, sometimes a prison uniform. We're "society," righteously doling out the requisite shame and pain. If social masochists require an audience to witness their disgrace, that's our job; we're there to make it *hurt*.

Wachtler managed to keep up the astonishing performance even in his post-jailbird years. Sentence served, social debt paid, he fashioned a new identity for himself. Or not exactly new: billing himself as a prison reform advocate, he took his abjection on the road, hitting the lecture circuit and beginning work on his version of the story, *After the Madness: A Judge's Own Prison Memoir*. In short, he devoted himself to reliving the degradations of his prison experiences, though this time around explicitly for an audience. Another man might have wanted to put those years of humiliation behind him. Wachtler had no such intention. Consider his rather detailed account of undergoing a strip search: despite knowing intellectually what a strip search was, he found himself unprepared for the experience "of being stripped naked in front of strangers, who then examine every crevice and orifice of your body. . . . I have learned by being commanded to strip, bend, spread, lift, and do a sort of naked and public pirouette that is beyond embarrassment."

Reliving the embarrassments of prison life may seem like a perverse pastime once the fallen eminence is finally sprung, but the self-flagellations don't stop there. Consider the form of the memoir itself, constructed as a now and then saga, thus weaving humiliation into its very structure. By juxtaposing anecdotes about inmate Wachtler's jailhouse life with decisions that Judge Wachtler wrote on the same issues, from strip searches to solitary confinement to conjugal visits, the book replays the fall from grace—the pinnacles of achievement to the dirt heap of prison life—over and over. "Take that shit out of your ears and listen!" a twenty-something guard shouts when the former chief justice—once responsible for running the entire state judiciary, supervising some three thousand judges and thirteen thousand non-judicial employees—doesn't hear an order. It's a nonstop carnival of humiliation and disgrace, but this time played out in cinematic detail for the benefit of a national audience, a naked public pirouette for all to admire.

Miss Schreber

Literature and theater are teeming with tragic characters who watch themselves act and who soliloquize on their downfalls, providing running commentaries (not always entirely reliable) as they flamboyantly self-immolate. Many of the greats have taken on this theme—Shakespeare, for one, knew a thing or two about personalities turned against themselves. But there's a more recent slice of literary history glimmering in the background of the Wachtler story, since it happens that Freud based one of his famous case studies on another eminent judge who also went mad. This was Daniel Paul Schreber, who like Wachtler was chief judge of a prestigious state appellate court, though his was in Germany a century or so ago. Freud never actually met Schreber, though Schreber's 1903 *Memoirs of My Nervous Illness*, a harrowing first-person description of encroaching madness, was widely admired throughout Europe and frequently written about, then and since. Freud was so taken with its acuity he joked to Jung

that Schreber should be made a professor of psychiatry.

I don't imagine that Wachtler knew of Schreber, but the similarities between the two are strangely numerous: both were Jewish, both suffered from bouts of lurid delusions, both had fantasies of persecution that, ironically, ensured their subsequent confinement, and both eventually wrote books describing their descents into madness. Their symptoms resonate too: disabling hypochondria, adoption of feminine personas with highly elaborate biographies (one of Schreber's was "an Alsatian girl who had to defend her honor against a victorious French officer"). Schreber also had his persecutor—his Chertoff—one Dr. Flechsig, the head of the clinic where Schreber was confined and, in his words, his "soul-murderer." Like Wachtler, Schreber had been a man of "strict morals" before his nervous illness, inclined toward sexual asceticism, though madness had the effect of ushering him into a feverish erotic reawakening. This included the overwhelming desire to be sexually penetrated "like a strumpet" by God's sunbeams, though they also jeered him for it, calling him "Miss Schreber" and making lewd jokes about his impending emasculation. Oddly enough, sunbeams figured for Wachtler as well: when mailing Theresa O'Connor's letters from New Jersey, Wachtler became obsessed with finding exactly the right mailbox and, in order to decide which of the several boxes was the right one, drove to New Jersey and waited until the sun came up and reflected off the boxes. "The first box the sun hit would be the right one to mail the letter in. The one that would give the letter all the right meaning."

Wachtler's *After the Madness* hasn't received quite the same acclaim as Schreber's celebrated efforts, at least not to date. As a writer, Wachtler tends to strain for literary effect—there are passages so laden with portentous symbolism that if Freud were still alive he might have been forced to write a coda to the Schreber case. Consider the passage regarding Wachtler's first day in prison:

> I was now joined by other new prisoners and, again stripped naked, was shepherded cattle fashion in a straight line to be examined by a physician's assistant. . . . It was then, standing in line with the undressed, scarred, and tattooed bodies of my fellow miscreants, that I saw it. The red snake. . . .
>
> This one glistened with the sweat of the inmate's back over which it appeared to slither. Its body was coiled and entwined through the eye of a skull—in one eye and out the other. . . . What had become of my honorary degrees and gold medals and plaques? All replaced by a red snake grotesquely tattooed on the back of a prisoner who would be my companion for the many months ahead. That snake would be seared in my memory much like the mark of Cain.

Freud being unavailable for comment, let me put it this way: Come on! Is there anyone on earth in this day and age not aware that snakes are an age-old phallic symbol? Is there anyone in this day and age unaware of the endless jokes about what happens to men in prison (which unincarcerated men across the land get a curious amount of pleasure joking about, one can't help notice)? The subtext is laid on with such a heavy hand, the language is so erotically charged (*glistened, entwined, sweat*), how is anyone supposed to read this with eyebrows unraised?

The memoir as a whole leaves the distinct impression that, for Wachtler, ending up in prison was the culmination of a lifelong journey. As we learn, he had an abiding fascination with prisons long before being forced to take up residence in one; anecdotes and references to imprisonment pepper the pages. Other accounts of Wachtler's career tell the same story: even in his first campaign commercial some twenty years earlier, at the inception of his judicial career, there's Sol Wachtler in a prison, strolling through the corridors, slamming a cell door shut for effect—*clang!*—promising to nab more criminals than his opponent. The problem, his critics jumped to point out at the time, was that appeals court judges don't actually deal with criminals, or not directly. Wachtler refused to pull the ad. (There was such a stink about it that the New York Bar Association finally issued stricter ethical guidelines for judicial campaign advertising.)

Once in office, as he himself relates, Wachtler made a point of requiring all the judges sitting under him to take regular prison tours: to Attica "while the embers of revolt still smoldered," to the notorious Sing Sing, to the deceptively bucolic-sounding Greenhaven, the alluring Auburn—the names savored like an incantation, like private poetry. Given subsequent events, these judicial field trips begin to sound more like real estate scouting than a professional duty. Wachtler admits as much: "Prison visitations are often made not out of concern for the imprisoned but out of curiosity. Before I ever thought I would be a prisoner, the fearsome aspects of 'the prison' only heightened my interest in visiting one."

It's sometimes speculated that certain professions attract certain personality types: surgery can be a sanctioned avenue for sadism, cops may be drawn to policing as a way to vent their own violent tendencies. Those with verboten fascinations do well to find creative sublimations in professional obligations (writers know something about this too, needless to say). When Wachtler confesses that he's captivated by the prospect of visiting prisons, his admission raises the possibility that a job in the criminal justice system might be especially compelling to someone with his particular preoccupations. At the very least, it's a socially authorized way to involve oneself in punishment scenarios without the stigma or self-recriminations that other methods might involve.

Wachtler also mentions that he'd once been a sought-after speaker on legal subjects, and one of his favorite topics was, no surprise, the state of American prisons. In *After the Madness*, he reminisces about one speech in particular, delivered to the League of Women Voters on his pet subject: prison reform. What he told the ladies was this: "Our prisons do not rehabilitate. The only thing our prisons seem to cure is heterosexuality."

And did prison cure Judge Wachtler of heterosexuality? His memoir, though rife with colorful examples of the day-to-day indignities of incarceration and packed with anecdotes about the motley collection of prisoners he encountered, is silent, other than this one quip, on the subject of homosexuality in prison. Though we do reencounter that portentous red snake, which manages to writhe its way from the book's opening pages all the way to the conclusion, reminding Wachtler that when he's freed from prison, his real punishment will start.

> When the designers of the sentencing guidelines were calculating their levels and degrees of discipline, they never factored in this harshest of all penalties. God did when He sought to punish Adam and Eve for their transgression. He chose exile. That is what I fear—a form of exile, or shunning, that will disable me for the rest of my life.
>
> And when God punished Cain, he did so by sending him into the world with a mark so that everyone would know of his shame. A mark that must have been very much like the red snake that I saw that first day at Butner.

Migrating from the naked inmate's glistening back to take up permanent residence in Wachtler's imagination, that Technicolor snake becomes both the sign of his own abjection and a framing device for the downfall story. The choice may be symbolically heavy-handed, but it vividly captures the complex way that erotic fascination and the self-prescribed punishment for it might be encapsulated in the same action, condensed into a single slithery image.

Given that Sol Wachtler will go down in judicial history as someone who became fixated on a woman and ruined himself over her, it also seems worth mentioning that the starting point for erotomania and stalking behavior—at least according to some who've studied the phenomenon, including Freud—is actually the contrary impulse. That is, an exaggerated heterosexual fixation—stalking, for instance—is a way of proclaiming to the world, "I don't love him, I love *her*!"—thus disguising a repudiated or unconscious wish with a showy public performance of the opposite desire. It's a way of deflecting the audience's attention: *Look here, not there.* All of which suggests, in other words, that the flamboyant "Look at me" element of scandal might be, in at least some cases, a subterfuge: that the punishment solicited from society is really meant, by way of an inner logic, to punish an entirely different crime than the one on view.

In this light, it's not exactly irrelevant that Wachtler's harassment of Joy Silverman wasn't the first demonstration of his propensity for playing out convoluted love-hate scenarios in the headlines. He'd actually staged a protracted, flamboyant emotional ruckus in public once before, though that time it was over a man. And not just any man but the Democratic governor of New York, Mario Cuomo.

Ermine Robes

Wachtler and Cuomo had been longtime pals and one-time poker buddies, back in the early days of their careers when Cuomo was New York's secretary of state and Wachtler a newly elected judge on the court of appeals in Albany. Despite belonging to different parties, their politics were similarly liberal, and they were also similarly strait-laced types—neither was much interested in the womanizing and cocktail parties that fellow downstaters got up to during their escapes from the nest—which meant they usually ended up having dinner together several nights a week. When Cuomo was elected lieutenant governor and the press started speculating that the two would end up running against each other for governor, they made a joking agreement that if they did, the winner would appoint the loser chief judge. Cuomo did subsequently run (though not against Wachtler) and indeed appointed Wachtler chief judge two years later, despite Wachtler's being a Republican, prompting speculation that the appointment was Cuomo's belated thank-you note to Wachtler for not having run himself.

If it was a thank you, there was definitely a backhanded quality to it, since Cuomo, whose indecision was legendary, made Wachtler wait until the last possible moment for the news. It was exactly 11:58 on New Year's Eve, the day before the swearing in, that he got the tap, Wachtler recalls in his memoir. When Wachtler describes waiting for Cuomo's call, it's with the nervous anticipation of a teenage girl hoping for a date to the prom. After sitting tensely by the phone all evening, shortly before midnight he gave up and got in the shower, he relates. A few minutes later the phone finally rang. Trying to appear nonchalant, Wachtler held off answering until the fourth ring. "Sol, this is Mario," said Cuomo. Wachtler tried to keep his emotions in check, wondering if Cuomo was simply calling to say that the appointment was impossible. Finally, Cuomo revealed his true purpose. "I'm going to do for you what I always wished someone would do for me," he said. The next day he'd be announcing Wachtler's appointment as New York's Chief Judge.

You understand that something emotionally consequential is being transacted here, though it's difficult to say exactly what. The same element of over-emotionality continued to color their relationship, which finally came to grief over that most common of couple grievances: money. In fact the animosity wasn't entirely unlike Wachtler's financial tangles with Joy Silverman over her trust. As annual budget showdowns between the governor and the chief justice repeatedly escalated into public vitriol and relations between the two deteriorated, Cuomo not only started refusing to take Wachtler's calls but also publicly compared his chief judge to a fishmonger who asks for too much and then settles for whatever he can get. As for

Wachtler, after five years of yearly haggling and feeling severely insulted by continual judicial budget slashes, he basically went off the deep end: he *sued* Cuomo in state court, meaning he served a summons and complaint on the governor who'd appointed him to his position. It was a flagrant public declaration of animus for a former friend and benefactor as well as a legally bizarre move—as one paper put it, "an unprecedented constitutional confrontation between the executive and judicial branches of the government." Cuomo's response was equally over the top and even more legally bizarre: he countersued, filing a federal civil rights lawsuit based on an obscure Civil War–era statute (he told reporters he'd been up late every night personally researching the suit), claiming that Wachtler had violated his rights. The state had better uses for its money than "buying ermine robes for the judges," he fumed. Ermine robes? It was the "clash of the Titans," according to *Newsweek*; "schoolyard gladiators," one of the

dailies opined. Everyone was aware that something was off about this feud; reading the news reports brings to mind the steamy male wrestling scene in Ken Russell's *Women in Love*: two naked men trying to get each other in a headlock for some not entirely specified purpose. In this case, it may have been psychic nudity on display, but whatever was being transacted was obviously a lot more complicated than the matter at hand.

So was the joke Wachtler liked to tell about the Hamlet-like Cuomo, who'd dithered endlessly about whether to make a presidential run. To reporters at a press dinner speech, Wachtler quipped that Cuomo was so indecisive that at his wedding ceremony he'd said to his bride not "I do" but "I might." Might what? the armchair psychoanalyst would have to ask. A groom's lack of decisiveness toward a bride is a joke with any number of possible subtexts.

Wachtler's public wrestling match with Cuomo was still in full swing when he started his harassment campaign against Joy. When he was arrested that November afternoon, he was also on the verge of announcing a run against Cuomo in the upcoming gubernatorial election. Two episodes of headline-grabbing behavior, two different grudges, two love-hate dramas—one involving a woman, one involving a man. Two alter egos—one a woman, one a man. And in the end, a life in ruins.

Whatever conflicting erotic currents or identifications may or may not have been crashing around in the dark night of Sol Wachtler's soul, it's worth mentioning that in the less tormented moments of his public career Wachtler had taken courageously unpopular stands on both gay rights and women's rights, arguing to decriminalize homosexual sex as early as 1972, when this was a daring line (the U.S. Supreme Court got around to it only in 2003), and accepting the endorsement of the Gay Alliance of Brooklyn in 1979, hardly standard practice for Republicans then or now. Or standard practice for the parade of hypocritical congressmen and ministers we've seen populating the scandal registers in recent years, so befuddled about their sexuality that they keep getting caught in embarrassing and often farcical gay sex scandals while inveighing against gay rights in their public lives. Among his other progressive stands, Wachtler also wrote a landmark 1984 opinion allowing prosecution for marital rape, so far ahead of legislative reform at the time that courts around the country began adopting it as a precedent because conservative state legislators wouldn't touch the issue.

The question Sol Wachtler did everything possible to side-step—in his memoir and in his subsequent interviews and appearances—was whether the bizarre fantasies and the weird impersonations *meant* something. His preference was to medicalize the delusions on the model of a tumor: some toxic foreign body had attached itself to an unfortunate host but had absolutely nothing to do with the host himself. Conflicts, needs, love, hate, erotic vacillations—all were struck from the discussion. He was a helpless marionette, a victim of bad brain chemistry, thus exempt from analysis. There was no need to look closer, no need at all.

By contrast, the fantasies of Wachtler's judicial predecessor, Daniel Schreber, have been routinely plumbed for every shred of meaning, picked over by generations of theorists and historians, especially those looking for insights into the political delusions that would soon play such a prominent role in the German national psyche. Nobelist Elias Canetti went so far as to declare Schreber's memoir the precursor text to Hitler's *Mein Kampf*—both infested with fantasies of omnipotence, both chronicles of paranoia composed in confinement. Freud unpeeled Schreber's psychosis layer by layer to argue that delusional structures aren't random, they have a buried logic that underpins the subject's entire mental life, determining both its content and its form. Schreber desired to be transformed into a woman and penetrated like a woman ("by God's sunbeams"), then had to punish himself for his desires. But it was the *intensity* of the defense—the intense psychosis summoned forth to mask the distressing desires—that signified just how profound a conflict it was. Defenses have an aesthetic character, Freud is saying, as if they were stage plays or screenplays—nothing about them is without significance. Even the tone is meaningful: when aspects of the delusion are humorous, it's an expression of derision toward the subject, the psyche's way of flipping someone or something off, even the social order itself. Recall the comic quality of the Purdy character, a nose thumber to the core. How random was the toothless Purdy?*

---

*Losing one's teeth is a common dream theme across cultures, by the way. Freud thought it represented castration fear (so too with the loss of any detachable body part), though in a 1948 paper titled "On the Meaning of Losing Teeth in Dreams," psychoanalyst and Freud disciple Sandor Lorand argues that dreams involving toothlessness are actually regression-fantasies, a wish to return to earliest infantile life, when the difficulties of reality adjustment were absent.

The current fashion for biochemical and brain-based explanations over psychological ones, for reducing episodes like Wachtler's to bad brain chemistry, thus negating the impetus for interpretation, would surely be a relief to the judge, though also completely disingenuous given the abundance of winks and hints he scattered in his wake: fat detectives, bad puns, red snakes, all strewn across the public stage like tantalizing clues for the rest of us to ponder.

Scattering clues so assiduously that he wrote his own arrest warrant, one might even say. I'm cribbing once again from Theodor Reik, who delivered a series of lectures to the Vienna Psychoanalytic Association in the early 1920s on what he called the "compulsion to confess," a syndrome that he observed in his patients and that seemed linked, he speculated, to some buried need for self-punishment. Reik's work keeps turning up in these pages because it overlaps with so many of scandal's essential motifs: it's an untapped gold mine of insights for the struggling scandal theorist, particularly his speculation that some collective universal guilt feeling is what prompts all this public unbosoming.

After all, confession *is* ubiquitous in human affairs: cops have long known that every time there's a highly publicized crime hordes of innocent people line up to declare their guilt, eager to take the blame. Everywhere you look these days someone's confessing something, not just in religious venues but in memoirs, the shrink's office, and, most relentlessly, of course, twelve-step culture. And let's not forget the tidal wave of reality TV shows, the genre in dominance at the moment, bestowing on lucky participants the opportunity to live their lives before surveillance cameras for months on end, while subjected to ingenious ritual humiliations and confessional regimes. One of my own favorites is a reality quiz show that has contestants confess real-life embarrassing secrets while hooked up to a polygraph machine in front of their friends and family members. One woman, who confessed to cheating on her cop husband and admitted that she wished she were married to an old boyfriend, won $100,000 for each true answer, then lost it all when, asked if she thought she was a good person, said yes. According to the polygraph, on this she was lying.

These confessional urges suggest rather dire conclusions about human destiny, thought Reik, surveying the far less intensely confessional landscape of his own time. If some gravitational pull toward confession and punishment under-lies the human emotions, if we're self-sabotaging beings at some subterranean level, then the future of mankind depends on whether we can succeed in reducing the power of the tendency since, basically, it threatens us all with extinction.

Wachtler concurs with Reik about the gravitational pull. "If this can happen to me, it can happen to anyone," he told Barbara Walters during one of his media appearances. This has an alarming ring of truth: after all, who *hasn't* stabbed himself in the back on occasion?

PART II

UPROARS

CHAPTER 3

THE WHISTLE-BLOWER

Toxic Girlfriends

The sadism of crowds is an endlessly complicated subject. Premodern audiences liked to watch their social transgressors getting publicly tortured and decapitated, or drawn and quartered with the severed body parts displayed around town, or sometimes disemboweled and forced to watch their own entrails being roasted over a fire. Then there was stoning—everyone gets to participate in the transgressor's death: the whole community does the killing. Thankfully, the modern age hasn't entirely eliminated grisly spectacles of public punishment—as Elias Canetti reminds us in *Crowds and Power*, "Even where stoning is no longer customary, the inclination for collective killing persists." Of course, these days we hurl punch lines in lieu of stones, inflict a social death instead of a physical one, thus propitiating the qualms of the modern conscience while still savoring the gore.

We turn now to the situation of the national laughing-stock: someone who transgressed social conventions on so many fronts that the entire country burst out laughing. Not with pleasure or peals of joy but in retribution, as a form of collective social punishment, and to do what laughter always does—release tension, mask anxiety, alleviate social unease. But what was it about this woman that provoked such vis-ceral derision, on such a national (indeed global) scale? There was an unusual confluence of circumstances, to be sure—a nubile young girl, a president—there were vast miscalcula-tions, but there was one decisive factor that clinched the deal: her face. It seems unkind to say it, but it was the face that launched a thousand jokes.

The curtain opens on Linda Tripp, a middle-aged divorcée with two children, working at the Pentagon in a midlevel job, someone who, upon learning that her girlfriend and co-worker Monica Lewinsky was having a secret quasi-affair with President and Scandalizer in Chief Bill Clinton, made a curious decision, a decision that rubbed the majority of her fellow humans the wrong way when news of it broke to the nation. After consultation with her friend and consigliere, a self-described Clinton hater and sometimes literary agent for right-wing authors named Lucianne Goldberg, what Linda did was this: she drove herself to the local Radio Shack, purchased a voice-activated telephone recording device, and began recording Monica's nightly phone calls, eventually amassing hundreds of hours of uncensored, rambling girl talk about all the usual female concerns—clothes, diets, hair, work, and Monica's tortured infatuation with a

charismatic older married guy who wasn't very available and insisted on having everything on his own terms.

You really have to wonder: as Linda motored to the mall that fateful afternoon, were there no second thoughts along the way? If decency failed to intervene, how about simple self-preservation—could she not foresee how this double-dealing would likely be regarded by the rest of humanity? Apparently not. As with so many of history's great betrayers, the forces that compelled her were beyond her comprehension; if any qualms were felt they quickly passed, and on she drove, to acquire the instruments of her duplicity.

And what of Monica, her young prey—not *one* tiny suspicion that her chum was capable of such a thing? No, like so many betrayed before her, Monica believed in the outward signs of friendship, which made her vulnerable, as it does the rest of us, but who wants to go through life suspecting your friends? Especially a friend like the stalwart Linda, so ready an ear, a pal indeed, whose clammy words of friendship would become an indelible part of the national record: "I *care* about you . . . you know, in my heart of hearts." It's a tale for the ages—two characters whom fate caused to collide, one the false friend, Iago in a skirt, the other completely oblivious to the possibility of being so hideously deceived.

Then a tender twenty-two, Monica was desperate to unburden her romantic secrets—and in what excruciating detail! Tripp at forty-six, though more than twice her age, was always up for a marathon phone session; in fact, she urged Monica to call her *day or night*. Which is exactly what Monica did, she called and called, never suspecting that her every phoneme was being magnetically preserved for the eventual listening enjoyment of the entire English-speaking world.

When she first got assigned to an internship at the White House, Monica had thought of the president as just another gray-haired old guy, that is, until she got her first taste of the much-renowned Clinton-effect up close. "I remember being very taken aback. My heart skipped a beat, my breathing came a little faster and there were butterflies in my tummy. He had a glow about him that was magnetic. . . . I thought to myself: 'Now I see what all the girls are talking about,'" she later reported to her biographer. (Staffers referred to it as "the full Bill Clinton.") Then came the thrilling glances, followed by stolen moments in the back corridor of the Oval Office, shared Diet Cokes and childhood stories—they'd both been chubby kids—along with exchanges of presents and tormented late-night phone calls. Clinton wanted to "be good," his code for not having sex, but he never entirely mastered the skill. Instead he conducted a lot of internal bargaining about what did and didn't count as sex, which would later expose him to widespread ridicule too, but it's not his scandal we're exhuming here (it has been sufficiently detailed elsewhere) or Monica's either (ditto); they're merely here as backdrop. Our focus is elsewhere.

Tripp, styling herself as the wise confidante, continued to provide counsel and reassurances, egging on the valuable confessions. In these nightly calls, Monica is variously tearful, complaining, angry, insecure, philosophical, and lovestruck when it comes to this not entirely satisfying yet all too absorbing affair with the conflicted womanizing leader of the free world. Bill would break up with her, then the next week there he'd be again, which is the kind of thing that can drive even mature types berserk. Many hours were spent by the two girlfriends on the phone debating various stratagems for getting the elusive Bill—forever distracted by international summits, third-world conflagrations, and standoffs with a Republican Congress—to pay more attention to the attention-starved Monica. Tripp offers helpful grammatical tips on revising Monica's love notes (better grammar was surely the way to the president's heart); she recommends a particular courier service to deliver the revised mash notes and gooey little love gifts to the White House (a service that happened to be owned by a relative of Lucianne Goldberg's who supplied Lucianne with copies of the delivery receipts). It was also Linda who advised Monica to construct a flow chart of her assignations with Bill, and Linda who pushed Monica to demand that Bill find her a new job—and not *any* old job, but one worthy of Monica's station and talents. Clinton's efforts to comply provided the basis for some of the more damning charges against him once it all went public, as it eventually would (could there be any doubt?), courtesy of Recording Angel Tripp.

At the behest of the Office of the Independent Counsel which was trying to nail Clinton on whatever it could find, from his finances to his sex life, Linda agreed to wear a body microphone to a lunch date with Monica at a suburban shopping center in Virginia. After lunch Monica was cornered by a team of federal investigators, informed about the existence of Tripp's tapes, and threatened with twenty-seven years in prison on obstruction of justice charges if she didn't play along (they also threatened to arrest her mother on similar charges). "Thanks a lot," Monica spat at Tripp once it sank in that Linda was the one who'd set her up. ("She said it like a recalcitrant little child," Tripp would later report acerbically.) The agents tried unsuccessfully to calm Monica down as she lapsed into choking sobs. "They did it to me too," Tripp lied, right to Monica's face, as if she'd played no part in the sting. That was the last time the two spoke.

Whatever your opinion of thong-flashing interns, no one deserves the years-long ordeal that ensued for Monica Lewinsky, which included amassing some $2 million in legal bills and having her car rammed on an LA freeway by photographers looking for a photo op, perhaps hoping she'd follow a previous paparazzi favorite, Princess Di, into immortality. In the end, Tripp and Lewinsky would assess their friendship's denouement in vastly different terms. In her first published interview, Tripp told the *New York Times* improbably, "I am so fond of Monica. I remain as fond of her today as I always have been. And I wish her nothing but the best." Lewinsky's final words to the federal grand jury after her compelled testimony: "I hate Linda Tripp."

I'm You!

Thus did Linda Tripp propel herself headlong onto the national stage; the nation took one look at this self-fashioned one-woman surveillance squad and instantly recoiled. The coinage *übersnitch* entered the vocabulary; if there'd been an American Stasi, she'd have fit right in. To make things worse, there was her own public statement to a horror-struck nation: "I'm *you*! I'm just like you," she announced tremulously at her first press conference. "I'm an average American who found herself in a situation not of her own making." The suggestion that we were all, each in our own unique way, Linda Tripps didn't sit well, even though at some level Tripp was probably right: betraying friends and their confidences isn't exactly unknown and most of us are probably capable of it ourselves under the right circumstances, much as we'd like to imagine otherwise. Still, in view of the eavesdropping technology, the calculated double-dealing, and the tone-deaf self-righteousness, it was a tough sell.

There were so many reasons to loathe her: the unremitting unctuousness and above all the hypocrisy, custom-designed to bring out the savage in the rest of us. Tripp's oft-repeated public explanation for the taping was that she was worried about being subpoenaed to testify in legal proceedings centering on Clinton's past sexual escapades—Clinton was in the midst of a lawsuit brought against him by a former Arkansas state employee named Paula Jones for allegedly making an offensive sexual overture in an Arkansas hotel room, a suit that Clinton eventually settled for $800,000, though not before Jones's lawyers were allowed to depose him and anyone he might have had consensual sex with, then and since. Which included Monica Lewinsky, they had learned. If Tripp was subpoenaed and testified one way in the Jones case and Lewinsky another—Lewinsky had already told Tripp she was going to deny the affair—then Tripp could be caught up in a perjury mess. She had to protect herself, and armed with her stash of secret tapes, at least she could confirm her own version of events.

The perjury worries had a convincing sound, until it turned out that Tripp had started taping Monica's phone calls long *before* there was any possibility she might be subpoenaed, concocting the scheme with the aforementioned Lucianne Goldberg, a political gadfly and inveterate schemer who was once part of the Nixon reelection campaign's brigade of dirty tricksters, paid to spy on the Democratic opposition. As it happens, Tripp and Goldberg had been hashing over the possibility of penning a best seller exposing Clinton's stable of sweetie pies well before Monica's confessions landed so fortuitously in Tripp's lap; they'd even hired a freelance writer to draft a proposal tentatively titled *Behind Closed Doors: What I Saw in the Clinton White House*. Tripp, who'd previously worked at the White House, claimed eyewitness knowledge of Oval Office sex shenanigans and was deeply riled by them; Goldberg just wanted to destroy Clinton at any cost.

But a book deal wasn't Tripp's real motive. She wanted the information about Clinton's sex exploits to come out, she'd later say, because the country needed *to know* that the institution of the presidency was being besmirched, and as a patriot, it was up to Tripp to do something about it. On behalf of the nation, she thus *arranged* to have herself subpoenaed in the Jones case (so much for the perjury worries), approaching Jones's legal team directly, on Lucianne's advice. Which is how it happened that she, Citizen Tripp, was the one who provided the lowdown on Clinton and Lewinsky's trysts to Paula Jones's lawyers, who gratefully deployed the information to sandbag Clinton at his deposition. It was the perfect perjury trap, as the Clinton foes financing the Jones lawsuit obviously foresaw; caught off guard, and fatally compartmentalized to begin with, Clinton stupidly tried to lie his way out. (As for the rest of the story—the second presidential impeachment in the nation's history, a Democratic loss in the next presidential election so close that it got thrown to the Supreme Court, Bush's disastrous war in the Middle East—please consult your history books.)

Patriot Tripp? No one bought it for a minute. If anything,

Tripp precipitated a national scandal so she could inject herself into the middle of it. Even less convincing was Tripp as Concerned Mom, explaining to anyone who'd listen that she'd betrayed Monica for Monica's own good, because Monica evoked the maternal instinct in her. "As a mom, especially with a daughter close in age to Monica, I would hope some other mom would do for my daughter what I did for Monica, despite the fact that it looks horrible, that it looks like betrayal." This last bit was particularly hard to take: being betrayed is bad enough, but being betrayed *for your own good* is really too galling. The problem with the after-the-fact solicitude was that it didn't exactly square with Tripp's performance on her own tapes, egging Monica on in the affair, then savoring all the seamy sexually exploitative details. Then there was Linda Tripp, Professional Feminist: "This was a young girl who, as an enthusiastic participant in this relationship, fell head over heels in love with the President. He clearly did not share those feelings and his callous abuse in discarding Monica Lewinsky made it look as if he thought of her as a servicing contract, a woman who could be easily discarded." That was the public version; in private she'd later be heard saying of Monica: "She was not a victim, she's had affairs with married men before." So much for sisterhood.

The problem with Tripp's self-justifications for betraying Monica's trust was that they were basically garbage. *She* didn't betray Monica, Clinton did; what happened to Monica as a result of Tripp's secret tapes was a far better thing for Monica than the callow abuse at Clinton's hands. She was

merely the *reluctant messenger*; the impeachment was a vindi-
cation of *principle*; the country needed to recapture its *national
soul*. The idea of taping had been *hideous* to her, but what
options did she have? Wearing a wire for prosecutors hadn't
been *her* idea. "People act as if what I did was tantamount to
murdering baby seals," she joked, in a particularly ill-conceived
turn of phrase. "All I did was protect myself, my integrity, my
kids." She reminded interviewers that she'd turned down
money offers for her story, which was true, but even if her
motives weren't financial, it didn't make them honorable. She
admitted to inflexibility and being judgmental—to being "a
black and white kind of person"—but insisted that she slept
well and could look in the mirror without a problem, another
infelicitous choice of words. "I have absolutely no regrets
about what I did. I would do it all over again, only better and
sooner."

What Lurks Beneath

You begin to see why everyone was laughing: the gulf between
Tripp's high-minded self-image and the backstabbing manipu-
lator she proved to be was a ready-made opportunity for indig-
nant humor and righteous digs. But there were probably a few
less savory elements behind the hilarity. For one thing, the
Linda-Monica tale offered the perfect excuse for misogyny: the
whole episode cut rather close to the bone (or claw) of every
gruesome stereotype about toxic female friendships—the
treacherous bitch costumed in female solidarity; the smarmy

girlfriend who courts confidences only to destroy you with them at the first opportunity. Who could listen with anything resembling a straight face to Linda lauding her own admirable traits when the subject turned to the (at that point hypothetical) possibility of her being compelled to testify against Monica?

> How do you think this makes me feel? I feel like I'm sticking a knife in your back and I know that at the end of this if I have to go forward, you will never speak to me again and I will lose a dear friend—someone whose friendship I value very much. And I—I keep my friends over a lifetime. I don't pick friends and then dump them when they're done with the job.

The lesson, all too clearly, was that beneath the feminist veneer women *are* still out to get one another, no matter how much we spout on about sisterhood. There perched Goldberg and Tripp, two aging schemers plotting to undo the luscious young girl, relishing their own ruthlessness, stewing in wrath. For reasons that are open to speculation, not only did Clinton's legendary charisma fail to work its magic on Tripp and Goldberg, they both took his womanizing very personally, despite not being called on to provide any Monica-like ministrations themselves. In what can only be called poetic justice, it later emerged that Goldberg was also secretly taping her own conversations with Linda, apparently wishing to preserve for posterity her every fiendish pearl of wisdom on the subject of betraying your friends. "*You've got to really rat, and you've got to tape,*" Goldberg can be heard on her tapes instructing greenhorn Tripp, who in the end proved to be a topnotch student of female treachery. It's difficult to characterize these two without succumbing to clichés like "bubbling cauldron" and "coven." Stereotypes about women have their pleasures: misogyny didn't go away just because public expressions of it are now slightly less welcome. Claire Booth Luce covered this same ground more than a half century ago in *The Women,* but it's still as fruitful as ever, which is why the jokes have yet to let up.

The truth, though, is that there was an even deeper cause for the laughter: Linda Tripp's face, which became an instant icon, a defining negative moment in American visual culture. By common consensus, it was ugly. As if in retaliation, the gloves were quickly off in the cruel-humor department: "What's the cure for an overdose of Viagra? Linda Tripp." There was tacit agreement that two decades of feminist language reforms notwithstanding, the word *ugly* could be applied with impunity and that the country's collective dispute with Tripp's brand of friendship would be expressed through jokes about her face. An "I Hate Linda Tripp" Web page listed over forty different ugliness jokes:

Linda Tripp is so ugly that when she joined an ugly contest they said, "Sorry, no professionals."

Linda Tripp is so ugly she went into a haunted house and came out with an application.

Linda Tripp is so ugly that when she was born the doctor took one look at her and spanked her parents.

Linda Tripp is so ugly her mother had to tie a steak around her neck to get the dog to play with her.

True, many of these had the musty recycled odor of Don Rickles playing the Desert Sands a couple of decades ago, like they'd been in comedy cold storage waiting for the right occasion to see daylight again, but other Tripp-inspired comedy was rapier sharp. One Web site reported the FBI's official confirmation that Tripp and burly Dallas Cowboys quarterback Troy Aikman were actually one and the same person; a bogus transcript of Tripp's bogus news conference confirming the dark secret mimicked the rituals of embarrassing public confessionals with pitch-perfect accuracy, especially the part when Tripp breaks down, sobbing, "I'm *not* a freak."

Then there were all the late-night talk show jokes (Jay Leno: "Linda Tripp told Monica Lewinsky in those taped conversations that she hasn't had sex with anyone in seven years. That means that at some point in 1991 some guy got drunker than any man in history"); there was an instant classic *Saturday Night Live* skit featuring a simpering Tripp impersonation by the 300-plus-pound actor John Goodman, in a dead-on blond fright wig (Linda to the waiter during lunch with Monica: "I'll have a Bloody Mary and two double A batteries"); there was a parade of pointed editorial cartoons in all the newspapers (the unbeauteous Tripp describing her television aspirations to pal Lucianne: "I could be . . . like this beautiful helpless older woman caught between these powerful politicians . . ." Lucianne: "Exactly! Attracting the soccer mom audience!").

Behind the welter of jokes and jabs about her looks, the country seemed to be groping for a way to dispel a certain lingering chagrin about Tripp's self-presentation, from her misfired demands for sympathy to her overly insistent coiffure. Yes, let's not forget the hair. With its big, blowsy blond ambitions of glamour and seduction, Linda Tripp's hair was nothing if not a case study in aesthetic disharmony, and when it comes to the semiotics of big hair, most of us can read the connotations, even those who don't use the word "semiotics." Hadn't we seen this hair before? In fact we'd seen it rather recently, in the presidential arena no less, perched atop the head of another gal with a recording device on her phone—a former Little Rock nightclub singer named Gennifer Flowers, who'd sold the story of her twelve-year affair with Bill Clinton to one of the tabloids for $100,000. (MISTRESS TELLS ALL: PLUS THE SECRET LOVE TAPES THAT PROVE IT!) Reporting on the media tizzy following these revelations, *New York* magazine put it this way: "The hypocrisy of it all was as obvious as the roots of Gennifer Flowers's hair." The jokes about Tripp's hair vented similar suspicions about hypocrisy, especially one political cartoon picturing Linda Tripp chomping down her morning cereal and chugging a breakfast martini as two helpful cupids buzz around her big bouffant: Special Prosecutor Cupid Kenneth Starr and Girlfriend Cupid Lucianne Goldberg. Ken whispers encouragingly in her right ear, "That pathetic Monica hasn't got a chance. He likes strong women who challenge him," while Lucianne hisses in the left, "It's you, babe, hang in there." The idea that at some buried level Tripp may have had a hankering for the charismatic Bill herself, that she might have *envied* Monica's dalliance with him, that a presidential impeachment had been propelled by the sexual disappointments of a bitter middle-aged divorcée, was too cringe-making a possibility to express *except* through a joke.

Pretty Is . . .

The role of beauty in the world is a subject deeply entangled in human affairs and emotions, not to mention a matter of consequence in philosophy, romantic love, and the cosmetics industry, but it's rarely a source of humor. Ugliness, by contrast, is the quintessential punch line. Ugliness haunts the realm of the beautiful, its banished and repudiated Other, something of a scandal in itself. To begin with, it's an intractable form of inequity: there's never going to be facial equality or a socialism of good looks. Nevertheless, the aesthetic judgments we pronounce upon those who fall short physically, by whatever the prevailing criterion, are brutal. (Both emotionally and materially: one study reports that those considered ugly earned 57 percent of the average income of those considered good-looking.) Everyone's aware of the cultural variability of beauty standards, everyone's aware of the emotional damage these judgments can wreak, yet we all level them ruthlessly nonetheless. Additionally, we who suffer by them pronounce them just as insistently—harshly judged one moment, harsh judge the next. As we all know, women both suffer more and are, at least according to popular lore, the harshest critics when it comes to other women. The point is open to debate if anyone has the energy, but even the staunchest feminist I know responded to the first news photos of Tripp by remarking mercilessly that she looked like a transvestite. Among the many problems with Tripp's face was just how inconvenient it was for feminist objections regarding beauty standards; in fact, liberal reformists as a whole came in for their own mockery in one political cartoon that designated Tripp as "physiognomically challenged."

Despite the unequivocal nature of physical judgments, the subject of ugliness has actually perplexed philosophers and aestheticians from Plato on. For one thing, no one's exactly sure what ugliness *is*. Is it a set of identifiable characteristics? Leading contenders: asymmetry, irregularity, things that protrude like warts or moles, and masculinity in women. But does ugliness reside *in* the offending objects and characteristics or does the power of ugliness derive from the instinctive response it evokes in *us*, from some unsettling psychological effect on the beholder? The ways in which ugly things achieve their ugliness are completely diverse, and if ugliness can't be reduced to the sum of its parts, how do we know it when we see it? Hence the definitional dilemmas: if there aren't a set of universal properties that constitute ugliness, we may know it when we see it, but what's the *it* that we're seeing?

Then we have the ancient understanding of ugliness as a morality tale. The long-standing connection of Beauty with the Good—a gift from the gods, Aristotle thought—means that ugliness must, by extension, be a form of punishment from the gods, a connotation that persists even now as a moral onus on the ugly. It's hardly uncommon to hear moral judgments expressed in the visceral language of physical unattractiveness and disgust: "That was an ugly thing to do," "That makes me sick," "Not a pretty sight." A premonition of evil or disaster lurks around ugliness's edges, a suspicion of moral and ethical violations: "Ugly as sin." If moral failure leans on the language of ugliness, then are the physically unappealing more likely to signify a lack of virtue and be held morally responsible for their aesthetic insufficiencies? When an editorial cartoonist drew a series of frames featuring Linda Tripp as a snake, a worm, a frog, and a rat, was it her actions or her looks that made the joke funny? Snakes, worms, and rats conventionally symbolize betrayal and bad behavior, but in our culture's animal symbolism a frog is just ugly.

Poor Linda, so perilously poised at the intersection of two indelible forms of social failure. Guilty of terribly betraying a friend, an egregious act in a culture that reviles a stool pigeon as the lowest of the low, and lacking the requisite allure in the visual department, she was the bearer of two varieties of social disgrace, each refracted through the magnifying lens of the other. No doubt the combination licensed the barely repressed violence of the jokes, the quality of atavistic aggression, every punch line like a hard right cross to the kisser. Though you couldn't help noting that physical attractiveness on the part of the tellers of ugliness jokes was not a prerequisite, which is curious in itself: did the jokesters think they were granted an exemption from their own aesthetic standards by virtue of Tripp's moral failures, or were somehow inoculated from similar judgments by the power of their jokes? This is either magical thinking or unbelievably optimistic, though when it comes to the subject of faces, nothing can be taken entirely at face value.

Needless to say, not everyone was joining in the laughter. Feminist spokesperson Gloria Steinem weighed in with the obligatory *Times* opinion piece detailing the differential treatment of women when it comes to looks and the dehumanizing effects on all of us, arguing that the country should be focusing on Tripp's actions, not her face. Tellingly, even Steinem felt compelled to describe Tripp as having been "born less than conventionally attractive"—note the sound of words being minced. But *was* Linda Tripp's face an accident of birth? Or to put it more bluntly, even if we don't start out by choosing our faces, do we bear some responsibility for them all the same? So the jokes implied, as did George Orwell, who famously remarked that by age fifty everyone has the face he deserves.

For all her well-meaningness, Steinem evaded the kernel of buried anxiety in the jokes, the troubling possibility that appearance and essence *are* hard to disentangle, that you *can* judge a book by its cover. The suspicion that what we look like reflects who we are has left quite a gouge in Western culture— from Homer's *Iliad*, whose ugliest character is also the most despicable, to the Brothers Grimm, whose bad stepmothers are wart-ridden hunchbacks (good princesses get golden tresses and pearly smiles), to Shakespeare's Cassius, to the Wicked Witch of the West. Tripp's ugliness turned her colossal betrayal into a gratifyingly mythic sort of tale, and the mythic is the conceptual grid that all of us fed a diet of fairy tales and *The Wizard of Oz* as children will be attuned to for life.

Linking character to physiognomy gets a bad rap these days, but it's a practice that's had its intellectual defenders, among them the nineteenth-century Italian physician and criminologist Cesare Lombroso, who thought that criminal behavior could be predicted by physical anomalies such as protruding jaws, drooping eyes, big ears, flat noses, or sloping shoulders. Surprisingly, there are a few modern criminologists still pursuing links between physical appearance and criminal behavior: a 1969 survey of prison inmates in New York found that about half had at least moderate degrees of disfigurement; a 1993 follow-up study examined the relation of "minor physical anomalies," or MPAs—webbed or extra toes, widely spaced eyes, and malformed fingers or ears—to crime. One hypothesis is that genetic factors responsible for MPAs might affect the same part of the central nervous system that produces problems like hyperactivity or impulsiveness, which themselves increase the propensity for antisocial behavior.

Despite such findings, the ability to overlook physical defects is obviously a sign of civilization's advancement; it's a good thing that we no longer send malformed infants down-river on open rafts and pass antidiscrimination bills instead. But beneath the thin layer of social politesse, the ugly and malformed are still held responsible for their fates, at least unconsciously. So are the bearers of what sociologist Erving Goffman called "spoiled identities" in his classic 1963 study, *Stigma;* these include both those afflicted by physical deformities and those with moral defects—histories of criminality, addiction, and so on. (Goffman was writing in a different era.) But Goffman—who reportedly stood about five foot three, so was perhaps no stranger to his subject— isn't the usual well-meaning reformist pleading for greater sensitivity. His more scalding point is that the stigmatized and the "normals" exist on the same continuum: everyone's been stigmatized at one time or another, and we all fall short of the ideals of physical comeliness sooner or later, given the univer-sality of old age and impending decrepitude. Anyone can play out either role, and those who get stigmatized in one cate-gory are equally capable of hideous cruelty about the stigmas of others.

As we see in the case under discussion: at one point Tripp can be heard, courtesy of her own tapes, mocking presidential daughter Chelsea Clinton as ugly, at another point telling the dieting-obsessed Monica that she looked fat in a particular blue dress, a dress that would later play a starring role in the Clinton impeachment saga due to certain incriminating stains. Monica was about to send it to the cleaners so she could wear it again; this was the last thing the conniving Tripp wanted, so she intervened with the unflattering commentary.

Engineering a presidential impeachment and jackknifing the course of national history is one thing; manipulating a friend with digs about her weight is something else entirely. Live by the sword, die by the sword—Tripp would hardly escape digs about her own poundage after launching herself and her girlfriend into the hot glare of national attention; in fact, both of them would spend the ensuing year frantically dieting once the media turned its caliper gaze upon their waistlines. Whatever degree of self-consciousness Tripp may have had about her body prior to what must have been a fairly brutal self-education at the hands of the nation's laughmeisters—she did later refer to herself ruefully as "hulking," though this was after she'd already shed a substantial number of inches—one thing is certain: every woman knows that telling a friend she's fat is a shiv to the kidney. Maybe it was hearing that remark that made me wonder if Linda Tripp *had* actually gotten the face she deserved.

And . . . thus deserved all the jokes? Here I hesitate, mainly because if something ugly in Tripp's character or soul or being was written all over her face, what does that mean for the rest of us? Or rather . . . our faces?

A Two-Faced Face

Psychologists who research facial expression would line up with Orwell: they tend to see a person's most characteristic expression—in repose or caught at unself-conscious moments—as a record of its owner's history. Our faces are our portable, visible biographies, you might say. Facial researchers typically break facial expressions down into regions—the eye and brow combination, and the mouth-jaw area—to study how the different districts of the face interact or, in some cases, fail to interact. Particularly under conditions of *self-deception*—falseness, conflict, or other competing impulses—the separate regions of the face can seem to be at war, one half refusing to follow where the other half leads. An ugly face, from this vantage, isn't something you're simply born with, it's an emotional distortion transformed into a physical one, an involuntary set of signals that tells a complexly personal story.

Having a face *is* one of the most perplexing aspects of being human: it shades every aspect of living, from self-confidence to love to your bank account. Like juries, we scrutinize one another's faces to ascertain whether the testimonies we're hearing are true, though often we have no idea what we're seeing: conflicting pieces of information flash by in nanoseconds, the details don't necessarily register consciously. We're constantly making assessments about character, reliability, even mate selection, based on these fleeting and minute signals even though we can't articulate why; we search the faces we meet—and live with, and love—for signs of what's "underneath," and whether this is paranoia or emotional intelligence or metaphysics, it's fundamental to how humans interact.

Suppositions about the existence of this "underneath" seem justified largely because the face is not a *voluntary* system, as everyone who has one knows (usually all too well): it invariably reveals more than you would like. You may intentionally smile at a comely stranger but you're just as likely to break out laughing at a funeral or to accidentally signal the contempt for your long-winded boss or oafish cousin that you're politely trying to conceal. Having a face basically means being a walking social gaffe waiting to happen. Everyone alive has probably been asked "Is something bothering you?" often enough to know that simply willing an expression to appear or disappear doesn't mean your face necessarily plays along. The blank page maneuver doesn't help either: having no expression is always a giveaway that "something's going on."

One way of understanding facial expression is on the model of the symptom or the Freudian slip: involuntary emanations with unconscious origins. Of course, we all regularly play amateur psychoanalysts when it comes to faces, reading the unintentional cues—"slips of the face"—on the visages around us; the play of conflicting signals and distorted features that result, like the classic Freudian slip, from some failure to integrate opposing impulses: I hate you/I'd like to sleep with you; I'm happy for your success/you're a complete insufferable shit. Note that to whatever extent we're able to comprehend the conflicted language of *other* people's faces it's because *we're* speaking the same conflicted language. It's the shared human plight.

Confronted with Linda Tripp's face, the nation scrutinized and reached the instinctive conclusion that something about it was just *wrong,* though it's only upon closer study that you can begin to say what. The mouth, as captured in photos, was either locked in a tight, rictus-like smile or, as in the early press conference photos, opened far too wide in a distorted Munch-like cry. The expression, typically, was aggrieved. In a much-reprinted office photo of Tripp posed next to then-friend Monica, American flag proud in the background, Tripp's lips are pressed together in a hard smile, but the corners turn down, as if something were hard to swallow. A pair of  oversize glasses shield much of the face; the rest is cloaked by that big mane of seductive blond hair. The hair says "come hither," but the face pulls back into itself mistrustfully. Monica's face next to Linda's is a complete contrast: the mouth open in a wide smile, the eyes a little scrunched together. This is what happens in a genuine smile or laugh: the eyes narrow, laugh lines appear in the corners—the whole face laughs. Tripp's face is a study in contradiction: the eyes, visible behind the glasses, are wide open and alert, staring watchfully at the camera, out of sync with the smiling mouth. It's a face in conflict, a *two-faced face.*

As the Tripp saga unraveled, reporters undertook far-flung archeological digs through the Tripp family history, which ultimately confirmed what most of the country had intuited long before knowing the specifics. Reports emerged of an angry adolescence, a philandering and subsequently divorced father ("He thought with his trousers," recalled a neighbor), a teenage arrest for theft, a troubled marriage to an army officer, and an eventual divorce of her own. None of the details was particularly attractive. In adulthood, Tripp seemed taken up with small injustices. There were reports of repeated calls to local police to lodge minor complaints; she was regarded as a "problem client" at her hair salon, treating employees rudely. At work Tripp was known to be obsessed with office gossip and other people's sex lives, especially male infidelity. CNN reported that it was Linda Tripp who'd been the source of an earlier round of gossip about the first George Bush's alleged affair with another Jennifer; Tripp denied it (as did Bush himself, along with the Jennifer in question).* Linda was someone who always knew all the dirt. Not just knew it but took it personally—she was offended by the "oversexed atmosphere"

---

*The alleged affair-mate, Jennifer Fitzgerald—Bush's assistant in Beijing and at the CIA, later chief of protocol at the State Department (the *Washington Post*, reporting the appointment, archly described Fitzgerald as having served Bush "in a variety of positions")—simply refused to talk to the press. She apparently failed to spill her secrets to any malevolent girlfriends armed with tape recorders either, though the affair was known in the press corps and later reported by Kitty Kelley in her 2004 exposé of the Bush dynasty, *The Family*. In contrast to the cannier Bush, Bill Clinton seems to have had a talent—even a drive—for choosing talky paramours.

The Whistle-Blower

of the Clinton White House though also weirdly absorbed by it. Perhaps she came by the vigilance justifiably: her father had scuttled Linda's mother and run off with his new love, then left the new wife for a neighbor. "He wanted them younger and younger," said another neighbor of Tripp's father, a charge that might have been leveled at Bill Clinton regarding the Monica chapter.

Tripp herself seemed to actively seek out opportunities for betrayal, perhaps to allay those old injuries, perhaps simply repeating a familiar pattern, though at least this time she was the one at the helm. She liked exploiting people's sexual secrets as social currency: it turned out that she'd boasted about the taping scheme to her four weekly bridge partners, even offering to invite the unwitting Monica to a Christmas party so the bridge group could gape at the presidential playmate. (So much for protecting Monica—but then it's not as though anyone had protected Linda when she was young either.) In fact, Tripp had a history of stabbing her female office friends in the back, revealing their confidences and talking trash about one to the other. Notable in this cohort was Kathleen Willey, a White House volunteer who'd reported being groped once by Clinton and made the mistake of revealing the incident to Tripp. In her grand jury testimony and elsewhere, Tripp contradicted Willey's statements that she'd been upset by the alleged come-on—according to Linda, Willey had *wanted* to have an affair with Clinton and been thrilled by his advances. As it happens, Willey had broken off their friendship before all this happened, after hearing from co-workers that Tripp had mocked her for being "useless." True to form, Tripp would later tell interviewers that she'd never considered Monica a friend either, despite the numerous protestations of undying friendship during those nightly phone conversations.

The Tripp family's talent for betrayal wasn't limited to the cheating father, it turned out. When Tripp supporters charged that Clinton forces had leaked information about the teenage arrest to the press, the *New Yorker* ran a story naming the original source: Tripp's former stepmother. This was a stunning disclosure: what is betrayal by one's stepmother if not an episode straight from the Brothers Grimm?

Was it somehow the legacy of this poisoned history that no matter what Tripp did, her own face betrayed her too, every single time? On the day the Senate voted to acquit Bill Clinton on impeachment charges, Tripp began a round of media appearances and interviews in a doomed attempt to rehabilitate her corroded image. Expensively made over and media-coached to within an inch of taxidermy, blinking madly under the weight of centipede-like false eyelashes, she carefully stage-managed every part of her new look except for one crucial element: her mouth. The mouth was a renegade, marching to its own drummer; it seemed to have an existence independent of the rest of her face and independent of the words emerging from it. When she spoke, her mouth did a peculiar thing: the upper lip reared up, exposing the top row of teeth, something between a snarl and a sneer. According to Tripp, her intentions toward Monica were *kindly, maternal*—she'd just tried to *protect* her. The tone was honeyed, but the display of bared teeth was a viscerally unsettling counterpoint. The worst moment came when Tripp was asked on NBC's *Today* show if she'd contacted Monica. "I know that I would not be welcome," she answered sadly, while the traitorous mouth flashed, just for a second, an incongruously mirthful smile.

In the vocabulary of the face, there are involuntary distortions; then there are attempts to overmanage facial expression, to present a *proper* face. Take the "false smile," something most of us instinctively recognize and generally react badly to, which we in turn try to conceal, probably behind a false smile of our own. What makes these smiles read as "false"? As purveyors of falsity ourselves, no doubt we all recognize when a smile is really a mask, a substitute that forces another expression aside— usually one that would reveal an aggressive thought or desire. It's not only the falseness of the smile we feel but also the exertion of withholding the truer expression from view. Beneath the smile lies a grimace—distorted and imbalanced features, a frozen unnatural expression concealing another one. False laughs, too, are a sort of compromise, a defense against the anxiety aroused by aggressive thoughts. *"I'm really a harmless person,"* they announce to the world. *"Look how I'm laughing!"*

Linda Tripp did seem particularly given to badly timed and badly executed smiles, along with false little laughs. "He emotionally abused her," she declared about Bill's treatment of Monica—and there was that little smile. There it was again when she was discussing Monica's current misfortunes, for which Tripp herself was largely responsible. "I would want to give Monica a hug!" she told Larry King, alarmingly. The smiles went by fast—you only noticed them, at least consciously, the second or third time you watched the interview. But the effect was subliminally jarring, even if you didn't know why. An actor portraying someone motivated by unacknowledged aggression would give a brilliant performance by emulating Tripp's syntax of unnerving smiles.

At one critical moment, the false smile dropped away. Asked by interviewer Larry King if she thought she'd played a role in reforming Bill Clinton's sexual behavior, she nodded her head vigorously. "I think he'll think twice about it!" she affirmed. It turned out that when Tripp wasn't aggrieved by something she had a completely different face, and it wasn't unattractive. The mouth closes, the lips are pressed flat, hiding that upper row of attack teeth, and she bobs her head. It's almost cute. Noting her crucial role in Clinton's supposed sexual rehabilitation, Tripp didn't look half bad.

It Was Horrifying

And why would the prospect of reforming Bill Clinton's errant sexual ways reorder Linda Tripp's features? Or turning the question around, what was her usual expression forcing the rest of us to see? In *The Expression of the Emotions in Man and Animals,* Charles Darwin argues that members of *all* cultures display the same arrangement of facial features for the six basic emotions—disgust, joy, sadness, anger, surprise, and fear—and that every human can accurately recognize these dispositions on the faces of others. Following Darwin's study of cross-cultural facial expression, researchers have come to believe that disgust in particular is one of humankind's most deep-seated emotions. Their findings tend to agree that a particular set of facial movements around the mouth and nose are central to disgust: primarily an upper-lip retraction, often accompanied by a nose wrinkle. If a raised upper lip is Linda Tripp's characteristic facial expression, the inference a facial researcher would draw is that some form of disgust has likely been her characteristic emotional experience.

What appeared to disgust her most was a practice common to many—in the King interview Tripp's deep revulsion at Bill Clinton's desire for oral sex came across quite clearly, along with her even deeper revulsion at Monica's eagerness to supply him with it. Why this should rankle her so much is less evident, but rankle her it did. Clinton's relationship with Monica was "a servicing contract," Tripp spit, upper lip raised, nose crinkled. It made Monica a woman who could be easily discarded, she repeated in various interviews. "It was horrifying is what it actually was," she told the *Times.*

It should be said that none of us, no matter how sexually hip or laissez-faire, are entirely strangers to such sentiments. No one likes admitting how much shame, embarrassment, and rage sexuality incurs, even when things are going well! Yes, we're supposed to have overcome all such pruderies, especially these days. Nevertheless, disgust is always just around the corner when it comes to the bodily; disgust patrols the boundaries of the self, especially at the vulnerable points of entry and permeability, namely the orifices, and women are the most seriously afflicted, say the psychologists. Why? As the sex encumbered with an extra orifice, psychoanalyst Lawrence Kubie points out in a still startling 1937 essay, "The Fantasy of Dirt," women are more prone to the experience of vulnerability, and in turn more prone to the experience of disgust. But an inherent squeamishness is something we all routinely repress, gender notwithstanding, though no one much likes being reminded of it. Tripp wore her antipathies way too visibly for our comfort.

The most paradigmatic forms of disgust for all human beings are those associated with eating and tasting and, of course, with bodily waste products; while anything ingested or excreted has a potential relation to disgust, anything excreted *and* ingested has a profound relation to disgust. Especially entrenched is "revulsion at the prospect of incorporation of an offensive substance," as the facial psychologists put it decorously. Things that remind us of our animal origins are also core disgust elicitors—body boundary violations, inappropriate sex, poor hygiene, also things that ooze. In other words, it's not very difficult to identify the offensive substance being imagined in Tripp's case, and sullying the Oval Office no less.

Deeply felt emotions come with long histories attached to them: Tripp was clearly no novice when it came to disgust, particularly of the sexual variety. Much comedy would ensue about Tripp's lament to Monica that she hadn't had sex for seven years. The reasons people don't have sex are as complicated as the reasons they do, though inbuilt disgust is the barrier to sexual intimacy that all humans have to overcome; it's the most universal of afflictions.* But servicing contracts and discardable women—here the language of revulsion gets more specific. Whose situation is Tripp describing exactly? By Monica's own account, the sexual relationship with Clinton wasn't nonreciprocal or without its enjoyments; it was also her choice, she emphasized. In her as-told-to biography, *Monica's Story*, she reports that before they kissed for the first time, Bill even asked her permission. But forget all that—according to Tripp, Clinton was "an equal opportunity philanderer," and she used that phrase a lot. His sexuality offended her at some profound level: he needed to be "held accountable," and she, Linda Tripp, was going to make sure he was. The disgust was written all over her face.

"I would want the adult to make it stop somehow," Tripp told Larry King, by way of justifying her unwelcome intervention into Monica's private life and national history. *The adult?* What an ambiguous formulation. When Tripp recalled her family history in interviews, her description of her parents'

---

*The consequences of an anatomical structure that positions the organs of elimination in such proximity to the organs of sexual pleasure cause untold psychological angst for everyone, as Freud is fond of pointing out; in fact, this distress was what he originally meant by the notorious phrase "anatomy is destiny" (now usually taken to refer strictly to women's lack of penises and the effect on gender psychology).

relationship also sounds more contractual than affective: "There was a pecking order in our house. Her job was to cook, clean, keep the five white shirts starched, ironed, and in the closet; his was to run the household, which he did with an iron fist." Her father was (like Clinton) a serial philanderer, apparently an equal opportunity one as well; he did discard Linda and her mother. When he left, Tripp said, she thought it was her fault. Despite the fact that her father hit her with a strap for minor infractions, despite being beaten down emotionally, she pleaded with him not to go, saying, "I'll do anything if you stay, give up my room if you want it," as she related to one interviewer. Childhood photos of Linda show an appealing little girl with a winsome smile. Her wedding photo has a wistful, hopeful air. But something had happened by the time she emerged in later life as our national whistle-blower—by then her expression had become truly painful to regard.

In some other world, Tripp's story might have had a claim on our sympathies, but in ours, more primitive inclinations supervened. Sympathy for Tripp would have felt too emotionally costly, it might have made her travails too proximate. Besides, she wasn't a proper victim. There was too much aggression in her misery: she was dangerous, playing hardball on a national scale. We *had* to cast her out.

New Beginnings

Restitution for wounded self-regard has been the motive driving most of literature's great villainy, critic Harold Bloom tells us. Let's not neglect its creative inspiration in the precincts of real life too, where it propels some of the best scandals. *Make someone pay!* Regrettably the real author of the ancient (yet still festering) wound is usually far gone, in the ground or frying other fish. Those designated to do the paying are just unlucky stand-ins, who happened by at the wrong moment when some misguided opportunity for redress presented itself. Emotional score settling is never an exact science, though it certainly makes for riveting public theater.*

Perhaps there's some aesthetic justice in the fact that Bill Clinton, whose political career was founded on his mastery of the close-up, should have become impaled on the grievances of someone to whom the close-up has hardly been as kind. If you're in a pitiless mood you might say the same about another woman who badly wanted Clinton to pay for his male privileges—at least that was the aesthetic judgment of the national joke mill about Paula Jones, who also flung

---

*And opportunities to rewrite history. Al Gore's loss in the 2000 presidential election was widely seen as the aftereffect of the impeachment: 44 percent of Americans said the Clinton scandals were important to their voting decisions; George W. Bush, who promised to "restore honesty and dignity to the White House" got three out of four of their votes. It may be unfair to pin the Iraq war on Tripp and Jones (there was also Ralph Nader to thank), though in mythic terms it's tempting to see it as the ugly woman's revenge: a cataclysmic virago-like world-destroying payback for centuries of inequity. The theme of the loathly hag continues in various reincarnations to the present day, says William Ian Miller in *The Anatomy of Disgust,* a fascinating tour through the less acceptable regions of the human symbolic imagination. Classically, the hag offers salvation to a young knight, demanding a kiss or sexual favor in return; Tripp and Jones update the terms of the story, though note the element of sexual nervousness surrounding these figures at every stage.

herself into the epicenter of American political life, casting Clinton as her personal nemesis. She too wanted Clinton to suffer for his sexual intemperance; unfortunately, her handlers hadn't bothered to mention to the less-than-worldly Paula what would be in store for her at the hands of the nation's comedians, who found the wronged damsel act less than convincing. Once again, everything that couldn't be said directly—class unease, discomfort about how class plays out in sex—got expressed through jokes. (Most notoriously by Clinton operative James Carville: "Drag a hundred-dollar bill through a trailer park, you never know what you'll find.") When Jones found out she'd become the latest national laughingstock, she tried the makeover route and, when the jokes still didn't let up, plastic surgery. Which didn't stop the jokes: "The proof Paula Jones wasn't lying is that her nose keeps getting smaller," was a typical response. The bad break for Jones and Tripp, the tremulous belle and the snitch, was being so myopically bent on exposing a male miscreant—as if that would rectify some ingrained sense of grievance, as if it would finally make them loved and admired—they forgot that exposure can be a two-way street.

In Linda Tripp's case, too, when a complete makeover failed to staunch the running jokes, she turned to plastic surgery. Turned to it like a starving refugee at an all-you-can-eat buffet: she had fat suctioned from her neck, chin, and other parts of the face, also a nose job and an eye job, all paid for by an unnamed supporter, she said. Having already dropped forty pounds in the first round of self-refashioning, she abandoned her trademark blond mane for classier auburn lowlights and

emerged a new woman. Or, if not exactly new, at least utterly unrecognizable. As the noxious Lucianne Gold- berg quipped to the press, a pal to the end: "It looks like she's had a head transplant."

It was true. Even for a culture addicted to the ethos of the makeover and habit- uated to wrinkle-free seventy-year-olds, there was something creepy about this new head. A *New Yorker* cartoon aptly cap- tured the national mood: two children at the beach digging a hole in the sand suddenly rear back in horror at the mon- strous rotting piece of detritus they've unearthed. The cap- tion: "Summer 2000. Children stumble on the remains of Linda Tripp's old head." You could imagine it stowed away in a closet somewhere, Dorian Gray–like, while an eternally fresh-faced Linda Tripp lures a string of trusting young maid- ens into her kitchen to stick their heads in her oven. *"Is it hot enough, my pretty?"*

If the old face unleashed an avalanche of anxious laughter, the new one was received with a certain shared horror. Maybe there was some collective bad conscience at play: the latest round of jokes was like a criminal's return to the scene of the crime—after all, it was hard to deny that the first round of jokes had been the reason for this counterfeit new face. There's a gruesomeness to plastic surgery no one much wants to think about, not to mention pathos: behind the glam new look were scalpels and incisions, blood and pain, and, of course, desperation—for love and approval and, worst of all, for prettiness. Underneath the veil of jokes, who didn't sense how awful this was? Who didn't hear the plaintive question hanging in the air: *Do you like me now?*

A similar frisson greeted the first face transplant a few years later in France, on a thirty-eight-year-old woman who'd lost her nose, lips, and chin after being savaged by her pet Labrador while unconscious from a sleeping pill overdose. Given the ubiquity of plastic surgery these days, there was a surprising amount of public squeamishness about this medical development, with various concerns tossed around about the psychological impact and the moral implications of having someone else's face. The macabre circumstances probably didn't help, nor did the fact that the donor was herself a suicide victim. The ability to acquire new faces in the surgical marketplace is provoking new forms of cultural anxiety, with questions about the basic ontological meaning of having a face hovering in the background. If you're not your face, then *who are you*? If people can acquire new faces at will, does this alter the human landscape in some fundamental way?

The ontological questions have yet to be addressed by facial researchers, though recognizing the degree to which appearance so irrevocably affects self-esteem and relationships, a few forward-thinking criminologists have proposed plastic surgery programs for rehabilitated criminals whose physical defects or general unsightliness might counteract their efforts at reform. In six out of nine prison studies, recidivism rates were found to be reduced by plastic surgery. Obviously good news for Linda Tripp's future girlfriends, should there be any volunteers.

CHAPTER 4

AN OVER-IMAGINATIVE WRITER

Duped

No one likes a bullshit artist, though we're surrounded by them—no doubt we *are* them: it's the modern condition. Who doesn't sell off little pieces of themselves every day? That's how it works in a market society; the question is how much you can get (generally not enough). You have to *fake it to make it*, as the saying goes. We're steeped in inauthenticity, which makes us yearn for the genuine: genuineness is a highly valuable commodity and anyone possessing it (or at least the appearance of it) can become a cultural luminary and reap the big bucks. Still, just "doing it for the money" raises hackles, it makes you a whore: a media whore, an attention whore—

new types of whoredom keep getting invented. Everyone hates a sellout (though not as much as a failure) because in the contemporary moral-monetary equation, market-driven behavior is coded as shallow and inauthentic. Except that we're all market-driven! Turning down money is a sign of integrity (it means you have principles), though of course we also revere those who've struck it super-rich—tech-bubble billionaires, self-promoting real estate magnates—to whom we turn for life lessons and character tips, even from those universally regarded as assholes.

In other words, the relation between the self and the market is completely conflicted and getting more that way all the time.

With authenticity sounding its dying gasps, we lap up stories of the *real* self and gravitate toward those with a talent for spilling their guts in public. Weepy TV tell-alls shepherded by tough-talking therapist-ringmasters, heartfelt memoirs of addictions and childhood abuses—these are the cultural forms in ascendancy, because what's more real than pain and shame? Especially when the gut-spilling leads to self-transformation, which is the only form of optimism left these days—the world may be going to hell, but at least the self can still be redeemed. Even though at some level we know (not being completely stupid) that the recoveries come on cue, the misery is wrapped in a publicity plan, and these yarns are crafted for the market, which puts their authenticity bona fides in question and makes those who peddle them profiteers and possible phonies rather than the genuine article.

So every once in a while we eviscerate a phony or two and parade their entrails through town on a stick, a sacrifice to the authenticity gods. The question is, which phonies to ream and which to revere? Such are the moral calculations of our time.

They were both great self-mythologizers; maybe it was inevitable that when they met, sparks would fly. By self-mythology, I don't necessarily mean falsehood, though that would certainly become an issue. Let's just say they were particularly adept at turning their lives into the kinds of stories we crave at the moment.

She was born into rural poverty to unmarried teenage parents, abandoned by her father, and so dirt poor as a child that she had pet cockroaches and a doll made from a dried corn cob. Her early years were spent with her grandmother who beat her with a switch when she misbehaved; there was no money for clothes, so she was dressed in potato sacks, earning her the humiliating nickname "Sack Girl" at school. At age six she was sent to live with her mother who worked as a maid and barely acknowledged her existence; there she was raped by a relative and sexually molested by family friends. As a teenager she ran away from home, was sent to a juvenile detention center, got pregnant at age fourteen and lost the baby. She's admitted to smoking cocaine and other self-destructive behavior, she's had ongoing problems with food—an addiction, in her words, and her "drug of choice"; she has problems with relationships and used to act like a doormat with men. Now she's a billionaire and philanthropist (our black female Horatio Alger, it's been said), runs a vast media empire named after herself, and is widely seen as the most influential woman in the world, dispensing wisdom to the masses, moving markets and elections, yet she still struggles every day with her own insecurities, the legacy of abuse and abandonment.*

He grew up in a well-to-do suburban household but was getting drunk by age ten, smoking pot at twelve, dealing at fifteen. By the time he was in college he was consuming, smoking, or snorting such prodigious quantities of booze, crack, pills, acid, mushrooms, crystal meth, PCP, and even glue that he blacked out nightly, threw up regularly, pissed blood, and had a constant nosebleed. He started dealing on a big-time basis; when he was arrested for possession, he beat up on the cops and was wanted in three different states after skipping bail. He was self-loathing, rebellious, and self-destructive: on his last binge he fell off a fire escape and landed face-first, breaking his nose, knocking out four teeth, and leaving a large hole in his cheek. His parents shipped him off to rehab

---

*Even her name comes with a legend attached. It was supposed to be *Orpah*, an obscure Old Testament character (sister of Ruth and mother of Goliath) but was misspelled on the birth certificate. It was a singular name to saddle a child with in the first place: Orpah was promiscuous, irreligious, and had sex with a hundred men before conceiving four sons, all of whom were giants; she was finally slain after hurling a spindle at one of the son's enemies, who threw it back at her, slicing off the top of her head. You have to wonder what kind of fantasies these new parents had for this child (and about the role of names in shaping anyone's destiny).

where he brawled with the staff and refused the pieties of twelve-step ideology; through a combination of willpower and the *Tao Te Ching*, he managed to wean himself off drugs and booze. Now he's a best-selling author whose books have sold in the millions. But he still struggles with the legacy of his past, especially the memory of his fragile, damaged rehab girlfriend, who killed herself the very day they were supposed to be reunited.

Some myths tell of fantastical events and superhuman protagonists, but ordinary events and mortals can be elevated to mythic status too, when the stories are artfully told and organized the right way. Humans used to wrestle with supernatural adversaries like witches or ogres; now addictions and compulsions are the ogres to be wrestled into submission. In lieu of giants and superhuman beings we have sagas of business titans and movie idols; our foes aren't malevolent gods, they're abusive parents, the destructive residue they implant within their progeny our version of the intergenerational curse. If we hear repetitions of these same stories over and over, if new genres are invented to transmit them (talk shows and recovery memoirs instead of folktales and epics), what remains the same is that cultures need mythologies to explore fundamental questions about the human condition, about the nature of the cosmos and the burden of mortality. We're all just trying to make sense of things the best we can, huddling around the warmth of our television screens and the flickering glow of our e-readers, wondering why the world is so full of pain.

She was Oprah Winfrey, he was the soon-to-be-disgraced writer James Frey, author of the blockbuster memoir *A Million Little Pieces*. She'd plucked him from the pack and graced him with her imprimatur (stamped it in gold right on his book covers—"Oprah's Book Club"), sealing his fortune and merging their destinies. As in so many mythic tales, their fates had been prophesied before they'd ever lain eyes on each other, inscribed—uncannily!—in their very names, hers subsuming his:

WIN FREY

They met on two occasions, before a watchful audience of millions: not on Mount Parnassus or at the Pillars of Hercules but in a TV studio in Chicago. The first time was broadcast under the rather suggestive title "The Man Who Kept Oprah Up at Night," though most traces of this show have since been scrubbed from the public record (a self-mythologizer's work is never done).* The few surviving fragments provide glimpses of a woman in the throes of seduction, or at least the literary equivalent. She'd been swept away by his words, she was gripped, under his spell: "The book I'm choosing kept me up for two nights straight, honest to goodness. I could not sleep. I could not sleep, people!" It was like nothing she'd ever

---

*"The Man Who X . . ." is a title device that itself winks at the mythification process. Recall John Ford's *The Man Who Shot Liberty Valance*, whose sardonically famous tagline, "When the legend becomes fact, print the legend" (referring to the role of myth in forging the legends of the American West), finds certain echoes in this story.

read before, it was transformative. "Everybody at Harpo is reading it. [Harpo is Oprah's production company, her name spelled backwards.] When we were staying up late at night reading it, we'd come in the next morning saying, 'What page are you on?'" In lieu of a Greek chorus voicing the community's distilled wisdom, there were taped segments of employees describing the book as "revelatory," some choking back tears, as was Oprah herself, who explained: "I'm crying 'cause these are all my Harpo family, and we all loved the book so much." It was every author's dream endorsement.

At the second meeting—official transcripts of this one do survive, though they appear to have been edited—she  unleashed the full force of her displeasure, having summoned Frey back to her sanctum when word filtered down of his duplicities: "I have to say it is difficult for me to talk to you because I feel really duped. But more importantly, I feel that you betrayed millions of readers." He'd lulled her with false tales and though she'd enjoyed it while it lasted—too much, as those gushing fragments reveal—now he had to be punished. She'd anointed him and he'd made her look stupid, spitting on her largesse and impugning her standing as a moral icon. Her fans were upset, the critics howling; it was a rare chink in the Oprah brand. Like a wrathful demigoddess, she had him publicly flayed, then cast off to the underworld of media ignominy to serve out the remainder of his days. The rest of the kingdom obediently complied: *Time* named him The Most Notorious Author in America, his publisher dropped him, his movie deal fell through, and he became an enduring symbol for the scourge of fakery and manipulation in American life.

Another long-standing pattern found in myth has to do with the driving out of the scapegoat. Scholars suggest that the scapegoat figure derives from a real situation that must have often occurred in early human or primate history, when a group of men or apes, pursued by nasty carnivores, were able to save themselves by sacrificing one member of the group. This pattern persists through time, surmise the scholars, because it's grounded in a basic human need—survival—and because scapegoats continue to be socially useful. After all, it's not like Frey was the *only* phony in town.

Exposed

When it comes to hitting bottom and climbing your way back up step by step (twelve of them, generally), the book-buying public can't seem to get enough of these inspirational little tales. Addiction and compulsion have become the privileged signs of interiority (sex addiction, too, a recently discovered ailment, along with shopping, love, and now the Internet). Once it was poets and novelists who mapped the dilemmas of the self; these days it's the prerogative of the recovered. Publishers cresting the boom dangle book contracts like nickel bags at a playground for manuscripts with titles like *Smashed, Tweaked, Crank, Broken, Dry, Wasted, Smack, Cut*—just a few recent variations on the theme. As you might infer from the titles, the stories can get a bit generic, with the typical narrative marching a well-trodden path from sin to redemption, abjection to dignity, failed self-mastery to insight and epiphany. The predictability doesn't seem to trouble the audience; in fact, these addiction tales can be a bit addictive in themselves, which lends the enterprise a pleasing formal symmetry: compulsive reading about compulsive behavior.

But I don't want to sound cynical or imply that writing one of these things would be a piece of cake. The confessional author has to be willing to confront the absolute worst in himself, down to the very dregs of his soul, then lay it bare for the rest of us, and frankly, we can be a tough audience. The judgments aren't confined to the author's literary talents or lack thereof; we're judging how he lived his *life*, we're judging his entire *being*. Confessing to having slept with your father will make you a survivor to some, to others a world-class exhibitionist for telling everyone about it. The despicable things you did while blasted off your gourd make for titillating reading but are also reasons for the rest of us to despise you. The now-recovered hophead has to have been pickled or polluted or pasted enough to have stared into the abyss but sufficiently clear-eyed to remember all the salient details, narcissistic enough to find every last crevice of his own psyche fascinating while remaining modest enough not to incite our derision. Personally, I dislike people going on about themselves in print, which usually reeks of covert smugness even when squalid things are being confessed, though let me add that I'm just as addicted to memoirs as everyone else: I read them out of voyeurism, then feel a little dirty.

The crucial thing, the sine qua non of the modern confessional, is that some form of *self-knowledge* must be acquired along the way: epiphanies, hard-won lessons, ah-ha moments—as all the screenwriting manuals advise, the protagonist must *transform* in some way, and who doesn't hope for a movie deal? But self-knowledge acquisition is no walk in the park either, as we'll see. A vast sea of platitudes beckons, into which inspiration-starved authors tend to fling themselves with abandon. In short, the pitfalls of writing about yourself are many and negotiating them is part of the gig: those who manage to succeed can become an inspiration to the multitudes, scaling the summits of the best-seller list, as did memoirist Frey.

Then a youthful 36, Frey had produced a swaggering account of self-destruction, criminality, drug addiction, alcoholism, and valiant recovery, along with a handy catalogue raisonné of his own bodily effluvium, in case posterity was curious. "I look at my clothes and my clothes are covered with a colorful mixture of spit, snot, urine, vomit and blood," is how the author introduces himself in the book's opening paragraph. A bit later: "Blood and bile and chunks of my stomach come pouring from my mouth and my nose. It gets stuck in my throat, in my nostrils, in what remains of my teeth." Before the scandal broke, all this had been lauded with superlatives like "electrifying," "compelling," "mesmerizing," "heart-rending," "vivid and heartfelt." "The *War and Peace* of addiction," ran another blurb. "Can Frey be the greatest writer of his generation?" queried the *New York Press*.

Apparently he could. "A gut-wrenching memoir that is raw and it's so real," effused Oprah, introducing *A Million Little Pieces* as her latest book club choice and propelling it into book sales stratosphere—two million copies in the next three months alone. Perched atop the *New York Times* nonfiction paperback best-seller list for much of the next year, it was translated into over twenty languages and became the second-top-selling book of 2005 (surpassed only by the latest Harry Potter installment), the fastest-selling book in the Oprah book club's ten-year history, and a major publishing phenomenon.

But then the troubles hit: after a Web site called The Smoking Gun launched a six-week investigation into the facts of Frey's life story, the book became better known as "A Million Little Lies." As the form requires, Frey had confessed aplenty, and to deplorable deeds; he recovered, he gained self-knowledge—in short, he kept his side of the pact. The problem was that some percentage of the deplorable deeds he confessed to turned out to be imaginary (though only 5 percent, according to him), which made him a figure of widespread ridicule and contempt—not for the scummy things he actually did, ironically, but for the scummy things he *didn't* do. Smoking Gun editors trekked around the country to the scenes of Frey's supposed criminal escapades, dug up old arrest records, and interviewed figures from his past, all of which culminated in a lengthy exposé titled "Oprah Winfrey's Been Had," indexing the book's fabrications, self-aggrandizements, and outright lies.

As the world now knows, Frey wasn't exactly the reckless, law-flouting desperado he'd portrayed himself as being—he'd never actually been wanted in three states and hadn't served eighty-seven days of hard time; he'd just spent a few hours at a police station. He hadn't actually careened into a gaggle of cops with his car and beaten them up when they tried to arrest him; he'd just gotten a couple of traffic tickets for misdemeanors. There were questions about whether he'd really undergone a root canal without anesthetic during his stint in rehab (one of the more gut-wrenching episodes he recounted), and his life-altering relationship with a high school classmate who'd died tragically in a train-auto collision was invented—the girl had died, but Frey had barely known her. Also, if he *hadn't* been sent to jail after rehab, this cast doubts on the veracity of his new memoir, *My Friend Leonard*, which took up where the first book left off, opening with Frey, a few days of his prison term left to serve, speaking on the phone to his rehab girlfriend, Lilly. This was the conversation that supposedly took place the night before Lilly, distraught over her grandmother's death—and because the incarcerated Frey couldn't be there with her—hung herself from her shower faucet on the very day of his release, an episode that lent the sequel its layer of tragedy and gravitas and deeply moved so many readers.

Pariahdom

"Lies, James, those were lies," charged Oprah, when Frey tried to defend the inventions as literary license. Following the Smoking Gun story, Oprah had initially stood by the book, even phoning in to the *Larry King* show during Frey's live appearance with words of support. ("Although some of the facts have been questioned the underlying message of redemption still resonates for me.") But now she was getting raked over the coals too; people were starting to act as though Oprah and Frey were kindred souls, like they were in some sort of alliance. Something had to be done.

Watching Frey's return visit to *Oprah* was like watching a dying insect writhing in a stream of bug spray—people who've molested their own children have appeared on the program and been subject to less moral opprobrium. It's not clear why he agreed to come back in the first place other than lingering self-destructive tendencies, though he and his publisher, Nan Talese, would later say they'd been bamboozled by Oprah's staff about what would ensue. Under the barrage of Oprah's accusations, Frey seemed resigned to his fate, barely even defending himself, though when he tried he sounded like a sniveling screw-up called to the principal's office. The best explanation he offered—and not much of one, everyone agreed—was that he'd developed a tough-guy image of himself as a "coping mechanism" and clung to it when he was writing the book "instead of being as introspective as I should have been."

Frey was going to lose this match no matter what he said. Oprah *is* the most powerful woman in the world, they were her cameras, her studio, her audience, and having built an empire on pain and confession, she owned this territory. Besides, he'd lied to Oprah, and you don't lie to Oprah. It was one of the great smackdowns in television history. To seal her inevitable moral victory and magnify the significance of the event, Oprah had also invited a panel of nationally known journalists on to vilify Frey for his deviations from the facts, though why journalists were the relevant experts wasn't evident: memoir isn't journalism and Frey's not a journalist. But Oprah was in charge, so no one pointed out the category confusion. No memoirists were invited on to comment, and certainly no one who might have bucked the rising consensus that Frey represented everything that was currently disastrous about America. Journalist Frank Rich said Frey was just the tip of the iceberg and compared his writing to the Enron corporation's shoddy bookkeeping practices.* For

---

*Not an apt comparison: the Enron debacle wasn't an individual foible, it was the logical consequence of decades of deregulation and crony capitalism. To be fair, the eroding line between public and private *is* one of the largest—and still unfolding—stories of our time, and a symptom of our confusion about what it means is the tendency of social critics to conflate individual scandals with corporate

columnist Maureen Dowd, Frey's books were equivalent to lies about missing weapons of mass destruction in Iraq, perpetrated on Americans by the Bush administration as rationale for a misguided war. The Frey-Bush equivalence had become one of those cultural memes; you heard it repeated constantly.

Clearly Frey was being transformed into a *symptom*: of cultural decline, capitalist greed, the triumph of narcissism, and pretty much anything else bad you could think of. He was The Man Who Killed the Truth. Though where did this leave Oprah, his former champion—especially after a personal broadside launched by *New York Times* book critic Michiko Kakutani, who charged Oprah with helping spawn "our obsession with navel gazing and the first person singular" by cheerleading the "memoir craze" of the last decade. Recovery memoirs in particular reflected the "waning importance people these days attach to objectivity and veracity," resulting in a relativistic culture that undervalues "the very idea of

---

and governmental betrayals. When married golfer Tiger Woods was caught in an adultery scandal, Frank Rich facetiously named him 2009's "Person of the Year," once again invoking the Enron comparison: "Tiger's off-the-links elusiveness was no more questioned than Enron's impenetrable balance sheets" and "Enron is the template for the decade of successful ruses that followed, Tiger's included." For Rich, both Tiger and Enron were emblematic of the same "flight from the truth" that led to the Iraq war—*and* produced the baseball steroids scandal, *and* led to the financial crash of 2008: "We were only too eager to go along for the lucrative ride until it crashed like Tiger's Escalade." The problem with equating a golfer's lack of transparency about sex with the failures of corporate and governmental transparency is the underlying premise that the distinctions between individuals and corporations and governments have been either erased or don't matter, which is simply specious.

truth." Kakutani never actually used the term *Oprahfication*, though it seemed obvious that's what she was talking about. Note that these "symptom of cultural decline" think pieces are not exactly a fresh idea—they're turned out on a regular basis by our more lofty-minded commentators. Working herself into Spenglerian high gear, Kakutani argued that the enshrinement of subjectivity and " 'moi' as a modus operandi for processing the world" had led to a litany of cultural low moments, including reality TV, the fact-warping films of Oliver Stone, Bill Clinton's lies about Monica Lewinsky, cable news, marketing hype, poststructuralism, Holocaust deniers, the imperial aspirations of the Bush administration, and the exhibitionistic use of the word *survivor* by talk show hosts to describe people coping with bad credit and weight problems. The weight comment was a particular dig: everyone knows that Oprah's been struggling with her weight for years.

Oprah's carefully stage-managed excoriation instantly transformed Frey into the most despised man in America. I may have been the only American who felt bad for him, though I can't say I was ever a fan of the books. Maybe it was the incongruous defenselessness of his demeanor—the bearish physique combined with a slightly lisping high-pitched voice, like a grizzly that doesn't pounce, despite all the macho posturing in print. (Or maybe it was that to someone writing a book on scandal, the idea that you can become a scandal just by writing a book can't fail to stir a certain fellow feeling.) He'd lisped a lot of stumbling mea culpas to Oprah and her audience during his return appearance, but there was no saving him; the ladies were aquiver with collective outrage. When he was an outlaw junkie they'd adored him; no doubt they'd all had their substance issues too, even if the substance in question was just excess desserts. But now they wanted to tan his hide, they wanted him thrashed to within an inch of his life.

Following the broadcast, reporters stationed themselves outside Frey's building day and night; he couldn't leave his apartment, this went on for weeks. He finally decamped with his family to France for two months, where, he later said, they have more sophisticated attitudes about literary matters and didn't understand the American fuss. The feeding frenzy continued in his absence, with pundits nationwide designating Frey "a sign of the zeitgeist" in thundering editorials and media tirades—it's invariably a blind spot of these pieces that those who write them never seem to see themselves as a part of the same zeitgeist. He was the triumph of postmodernism, an emblem for every form of inauthenticity; he was even inveighed against in an unsigned *New York Times* editorial— you'd have thought he was Idi Amin and had ravaged a country, that he had a nation's blood on his hands.

Irrevocable Injuries

So why *did* everyone go so berserk about Frey; why did everyone take it all so *personally*? In an unprecedented expression of consumer outrage, readers around the country claimed they'd been irrevocably damaged by the revelations about *AMLP*, as if the book were a faulty medical treatment that had resulted in tragically impaired lives. These really were some delicate souls! Class action lawyers around the country, sniffing dollars and headlines, launched a flurry of state and federal lawsuits that Frey's publisher didn't bother to contest, instead setting aside $2.35 million to settle the claims, over half of which went to the lawyers who'd instigated the suits and for court costs; all the damaged readers got was a purchase price refund. In the end, only 1,729 readers actually filed for refunds (totaling $27,348) out of over four million books sold, though to receive a refund customers had to sign a sworn statement saying they'd bought Frey's book because they believed it was a *memoir*. For all the uproar, it continued to sell briskly, an additional 93,000 copies in the seven months after the Smoking Gun story; in other words, everyone involved was cleaning up royally, despite the settlement. The fact that readers were still buying the book was seen as another count against Frey: he wasn't just a profiteer and a phony, he'd profited again from the scandal about his phoniness, which made him even more of a jerk.

Still, why *was* Frey the one being thrown to the wolves? He's hardly the first memoirist to play loose with facts— fictionalized memoirs are such a regular occurrence they're practically a subgenre. It's not exactly a secret that autobiographers have never been paragons of objectivity and truth. George Orwell somewhere remarks that autobiography is the most outrageous form of fiction. Ernest Hemingway prefaced his memoir, *A Moveable Feast*: "If the reader prefers, this book may be regarded as fiction." "All autobiographies are lies," said George Bernard Shaw. Here's literary critic Henry Louis Gates on the subject: "What the ideologues of authenticity cannot quite come to grips with is that fact and fiction have always exerted a reciprocal effect on each other. However truthful you set out to be, your autobiography is never unmediated by literary structures of expression."* Frey was following in a distinguished tradition: the history of literary criticism contains volumes of reflection on the extent to which memoirs prevaricate, beginning with the earliest examples of the form. Consider Stephen Spender (1909–95) on Rousseau's *Confessions* (published in 1782): "Of course Rousseau does not tell the truth. There is a lie concealed within his very method." The ambiguities continue to our day: interviews with contemporary memoirists collected in *The Autobiographer's Handbook* describe a series of hedges and stratagems for conveying reality, including eliding, combining, and reordering events, with complete disagreement about where the line should be. All memoirists reconstruct or invent dialogue yet enclose it within factuality-implying quotation marks, meaning the codes of fiction pervade virtually every memoir ever written, no matter how scrupulous the author claims to be about sticking

---

*Interestingly, Gates was writing here about a previous memoir scandal involving Oprah, concerning a critically acclaimed book called *The Education of Little Tree*, first published in 1976, supposedly by a writer named Forrest Carter about his relationship with his Cherokee grandparents. Celebrating its "spiritual truths," Oprah promoted the book on her show in the 1990s and later on her Web site. (It was also the basis of a 1997 movie.) *Little Tree* turned out to have been written by a former Ku Klux Klan member named Asa Earl Carter.

to the facts. Frey himself subsequently inserted a disclaimer at the front of the book announcing that some incidents were fictionalized, though it was not one phrased to appease his critics. ("I believe, and I understand others strongly disagree, that memoir allows the writer to work from memory instead of from a strict journalistic or historical standard. It is about impression and feeling, about individual recollection.) My own view, to put it on the table, is that when memoirists start declaring how truthful they've been, check for your wallet. Poet and memoirist Mark Doty puts it more elegantly: "It's a childish version of ethics to simply declare that it's wrong to make things up, and it seems like far too easy a position to claim that what makes a memoir ethical is that it's factually accurate."

Doty's position was not, needless to say, the mainstream view: the prevailing belief was that Frey had betrayed not just his readers but Truth writ large and deserved a hideous form of punishment. His defenders were few. But to be fair to Frey, he'd always been excruciatingly frank about his literary ambitions, and literature *is* a medium of imagination. He was quoted on numerous occasions to the effect that he didn't want to be read as an addiction specialist, and the author-heroes he invoked as precedents—Kerouac, Bukowski, Mailer, Miller, Hemingway—were literary bad boys all. Also hard drinking types who'd cut wide swathes through the demi-mondes of their time, many of whom were also known for creating semifictive first-person personas, mingling facts and fiction with aplomb as if writers had all the freedom in the world and writing was about carving out spaces of freedom, not adhering to someone else's conventions or literary niceties.

Faithful to his ill-mannered forebears and the wild-man persona he was either cultivating or didn't bother to suppress, Frey also gave a lot of boorish prepublication interviews announcing that he wanted to be the voice of his generation and head-butting anyone he saw as competition: "I don't give a fuck what Jonathan Safran whatever-his-name does or what David Foster Wallace does. I don't give a fuck what any of those people do." Of Dave Eggers: "A book that I thought was mediocre was being hailed as the best book written by the best writer of my generation. Fuck that. And fuck him and fuck anybody who says that. I don't give a fuck what they think about me. I'm going to try to write the best book of my generation and I'm going to try to be the best writer." In other words, he may have been an ambitious blowhard and too big for his britches, but he never tried to *hide* it: he flourished his tattoos, played up the bad boy 'tude, and the fans loved it. His agent (who would later drop him) called him "authentic." The media loved it too, of course, and kept coming back for more—they hadn't seen one of these for a while; even the reliably lunatic Mailer had become a bit sedate in his dotage. But what part were the rest of us being asked to play in this carnival of grandstanding self-abasement?

Scandalizers and their audience always share a certain complicity, but it was especially pronounced in the scandal over *A Million Little Pieces* since, when you actually read it, the premise that this book should be taken as strictly factual becomes difficult to sustain. With its flashy tough-guy stylistics, the mock heroics, its mishmash of abjection and pretension, this is clearly not reportage. The writing is stylized in the extreme: there are no quotation marks or paragraph indentations, and paragraphs lean toward a single sentence. Random words are capitalized midline (Jail, Garage, Criminal, Fury), an eccentric, self-consciously literary device. It's a book that screams Author at Work straining to write *literature*, which makes the apoplexy over revelations of literary license hard to sympathize with, especially since it's the book's literary qualities, heavy-handed though they are, that give the writing its jolt of the real, its sense of immediacy. If Frey, an aspiring novelist, harnessed himself to the engine of the recovery narrative to get his story into print, his readers compromised themselves too, swallowing his writerly affectations like pills mashed up in applesauce, so eager for a fix of recovery lit that the eye-blinking grandiosities barely registered. Root canal *without anesthetic*? Wanted in *how many* states?

Afterward Frey's readers were angry at everyone but themselves, angry as marks who refuse to admit it was their own credulity that got them rooked. Or in this case, their need to believe in the mythology of self-transformation, perhaps. And did those 1,729 irrevocably damaged readers who signed statements attesting to their belief in the factuality of memoirs pause to conduct a thorough reckoning with the truth status of these contemporary folktales or the fantastical elements of Frey's tales, or had they been willing to overlook a few ambiguities to preserve a necessary fantasy?

Despite the near-universal agreement that he was "a lying sack of shit" (I'm quoting from the blogosphere), the irony is that Frey *was* truthful: the truth is that he has a propensity to self-romanticize and, true to himself, that's what he did. He described himself in *AMLP*—factually—as a liar, a cheater, and an addict: "Lying became part of my life. I lied if I needed to lie to get something or get out of something." Was it Frey's fault if his readers failed to take him at his word? One of the more tenuous precepts of confessional culture is that confessing to things obviates them, that it's synonymous with self-transformation, as if recovery makes Abe Lincolns out of every former drunk and junkie. This doesn't appear to be the case. Nevertheless—and once again, true to his claims—Frey *was* a badass and a criminal, it's just that his crimes were primarily against literary protocols. He didn't flout the law, at least not to the extent he'd bragged about; he flouted readers who confuse memoirs with journalism. He brought social wrath down upon himself not for being a self-destructive, vomity drug addict—that part was fine with everyone—but for exposing the inherent manipulations at the heart of the recovery genre, though it's possible this was unwitting on his part.

Marketing the Self

Scandal specializes in revealing open secrets, so here's one to consider: writers write for the marketplace. If they don't, they don't get published, increasingly so these days, given the corporatization of publishing and the demand for increased profits.

The bottom line mentality was reflected in Frey's own publishing experience: when his agent tried to sell the book as a novel, submitting it to seventeen publishers, no one would buy it. When she added that it was based on his own story, he got offers—an unknown recovery memoirist looked like a more commercial prospect than an unknown first-time novelist, even though it was basically the same story.

In the aftermath of the scandal Frey told the few interviewers he agreed to speak to that he'd signed a non-disclosure agreement with his publisher and couldn't discuss the editorial process or why no disclaimer had been included in earlier versions of the book. He did, however, give one early interview to a British paper, claiming that he'd been told by someone at the press that if the book was 85 percent true, that would be acceptable. The idea that no one at the publishing house knew it was a manipulated manuscript was "absurd," he said, since during the editing process, time lines shifted, characters got erased, and segments were rearranged. Thanks to those assiduous Smoking Gun editors we all now have reasons to doubt Frey's adherence to factuality, but the existence of a non-disclosure agreement with his publisher would seem to speak for itself.*

Yes, Frey produced books the marketplace wanted instead of the novels he wanted to write (and based on his

---

*His book editor (labeled "James Frey's Enabler" by *New York* magazine) disavowed his role in the process and claimed he was working on the understanding that every fact was accurate—of course, his own reputation was also on the line once the fabrications were exposed.

sales figures, he wrote *exactly* the book the marketplace wanted) and from a commercial standpoint they were vast successes. In business lingo, Frey could be seen as a product innovator: he aligned the novel and the recovery narrative, reinvigorating the form and reaping the rewards. His critics thought he should have adhered to some pre-corporate code of honor instead, rejecting success in a grand romantic gesture, as if writers were exempt from the pressures of commerce, as if it were up to Frey to singlehandedly contest the forces of market capitalism. Maybe so. But here's a question: Do any of us?

We *all* tailor ourselves to the requirements of the marketplace (some of us more vigorously than others, no doubt), but no one's exempt from this social process, however much we desperately want to think ourselves uncorrupted by it. There's also no doubt that the increasing pervasiveness of market forces (and the increasing vulnerability of the citizenry *to* market forces) has changed the nature of the narratives we construct, and reshaped our mythologies of the self. It's not coincidental that the craving for life stories (and the popularity of abuse stories of every kind), not to mention this intensified demand for authenticity and self-transparency, comes as commercialism is pervading every last remaining non-commercialized enclave of existence, including the deepest corners of inner life. Or that the theme of so many of these life stories is the salve of various addictive substances. There are lengthier arguments that could be inserted here about the addictive personality as an advantageous social type for a consumer society such as ours—it's been said that every society produces the specific character traits it needs to sustain its particular economic forms: the Protestant work ethic drove the spirit of early capitalism, ours produces self-absorbed personality types who live to shop. The turn toward memoir may get chalked up to narcissism run amok by critics like Kakutani, as just another sign of a culture turned inward toward its navel, but recall that the cult of the self, from nineteenth-century Romanticism on, has always been a response to its threatened eclipse by industrialization. Narcissism may be our fate, but it's not an individual pathology alone, it's a cultural tendency, maddening as the individual forms it takes can be. (Interestingly, the narcissists are always *other* people.)

The Hungry Self

Speaking of tailoring yourself to the market, what about Frey's great champion, Oprah, our undisputed purveyor-in-chief of authenticity and truths of the self? She too specializes in public admissions about her various self-defeating tendencies and substance issues, though as it happens the substance in her case is the one drug James Frey doesn't mention: food. The entire country watches her battle with her poundage, which is also an intrinsic part of her public identity: no doubt some creative economist will soon discover a way to use these ups and downs as an economic indicator, as they once pegged hemlines to the stock market. Her fans suffer the humiliations and triumphs along with her, understanding that it's not a matter of caloric intake alone, it's an inner struggle—childhood demons, the burden of history—settled infuriatingly on her hips. But the weight problem also signals how much like *us* she remains despite the mansions and private jets—she may be a billionaire, but she can't cram herself into a size two either. (And by "us" I mean me—please let me add that having been a fat teenager myself, I'm no stranger to this particular theater of shame.)

It must be said that Oprah encourages this fascination in not particularly subtle ways: after one dramatic weight loss she actually dragged a wagon loaded with sixty-seven pounds of fat on stage with her to tout her victory. The slimmed-down Oprah is also a bit of a sexpot—it was one tight-fitting outfit after another after the last big weight loss; she even bared her midriff on the cover of *O: The Oprah Magazine,* where she appears each month in a new outfit and hairdo. But as usually happens, the months went by and you couldn't help noticing that Oprah was starting to look a little dumpier; the outfits became less formfitting, a double chin was forming. Not entirely a bad thing: her viewers draw solace from her struggles, her failures ease the sting of their own—it's said that her ratings are highest when she's the heaviest.

Though Oprah has yet to produce her own much-awaited memoir, the Oprah brand requires periodic confessions, and one of the more notable was a first-person cover story for the January 2009 issue of *O,* titled "How Did I Let This Happen Again?" in which she confessed her humiliation that, having dieted down to a relatively svelte 160, she'd now gained over forty pounds—"Yes, you're adding correctly," she lamented, "the dreaded 2-0-0"—and the reason subscribers hadn't seen her in a head-to-toe cover shot all year was because she couldn't bear to be seen. Such is Oprah's role in the culture that the story was reported as breaking news. I first heard about it on CNN (while at the gym, of course); it was soon picked up by all the major papers, boosting single-copy sales of that issue of *O* to over a million copies, the best-selling issue in three years. As Oprah knows, the marketplace craves infusions of shame: it's the most direct route to the true self.

Shamed she may have been, which doesn't mean the confession wasn't also rather artfully constructed. Let's start with the we're-just-girlfriends tone, skillfully calculated to hit us where we hurt. "You know how bad you feel when you have a special event . . ." "You have to figure out how to hold in your stomach all night and walk backward out of the room . . ." "What's true for every one of you is also true for me." Anyone who's ever had a weight problem has to love her for the pained admission "I feel like a fat cow." The grammatical tense throughout was the first-person abject: "I'm mad at myself. I'm embarrassed," "I felt completely defeated," "I thought, 'I give up. Fat wins,'" "I was so frustrated," "I think I hit bottom." The self-mockery has the familiar twang of your own internal monologues: "I was so sure, I was even cocky." You feel on reading this that you're in the presence of a real person, a fellow sufferer, even while knowing intellectually that it's branding: the cozy buttonholing language of merchandising, the personality as product. (I may be able to analyze it, but that doesn't mean it doesn't work on me—I even feel bad calling it calculated; it's like dissing a friend.)

The story went like this. Oprah's weight had been creeping up, in part because various health problems made exercising a problem. Having thought she'd overcome her lifelong eating problems, having made such a public splash about it, she now finds the scale telling her she hasn't. Self-loathing ensues: she can't believe she's let this happen, that after all these years she's *still* talking about her weight. But she is. She looks back at her thinner self and mocks her previous self-assurance, now revealed as sheer self-delusion: "I had the nerve to say to friends who were struggling, 'All you have to do is work out harder and eat less! Get your 10,000 steps in! None of that starchy stuff!'"

There are trips to various doctors. One finally diagnoses hyperthyroidism (an overactive thyroid) that turned into hypothyroidism (a sluggish metabolism that causes fatigue and weight gain). After years of thinking lack of willpower was to blame for her weight problems, at least now she has a medical excuse—this she says with bitter irony. At the same time, the diagnosis itself is so frustrating (thyroid meds can cause weight gain) that she starts eating everything in sight: "I use food for the same reasons an addict uses drugs: to comfort, to soothe, to ease stress." She switches doctors and medications but keeps gaining weight.

One day a friend tells her she seems depressed: "I think something's wrong. You're listless. . . . There's no sparkle in your eyes. I think you're in some sort of depression.'" So Oprah goes *off* all her medications and embarks on a program of self-healing—vacations, sleep and exercise, soy milk, vitamins and flaxseed, allowing her body to restore itself. (Just the mention of soy created a huge flap—soy is regarded by many in the thyroid-impaired community as practically toxic.) Another friend tells her, "Your overweight self doesn't stand before you craving food. She's craving love." This leads to an epiphany: "What I've learned this year is that my weight issue isn't about eating less or working out harder, or even about a malfunctioning thyroid. It's about my life being out of balance, with too much work and not enough play, not enough time to calm down. I let the well run dry." The problem, she now realizes, is that she doesn't know how to take *care* of herself: "I don't have a weight problem—I have a self-care problem that manifests through weight." And the moral: "Dare I, dare all of us give ourselves all the love and care we need to be healthy, to be well, and to be whole?" Oprah's conclusion: "I'm gonna try."

Now all this is as tangled as a plate of low-carb linguini: with all respect to Oprah, the closer you look the less sense it makes. Not only does the connection between her thyroid and the weight gain turn out to be a red herring, the thyroid problem simply disappears, cured through epiphanies about sleep and balance. The weight issue itself, initially presented as a source of gut-wrenching shame (and the hook for the article) also vanishes, solved by more epiphanies: "My goal isn't to be thin. My goal is for my body to be the weight it can hold—to be strong and healthy and fit, to be itself. My goal is to learn to embrace this body and to be grateful every day for what it has given me."

Notice the heavy lifting behind the faux-breezy tone—that "gonna" tries a bit too hard, like a politician working the room. And what else can we learn about the modern confessional from reading a master of the form? Most importantly, that every pained public admission is an epiphany-in-the-making. It doesn't matter what's being confessed; it doesn't matter whether the solution is coherent. What matters is the bond forged with the audience though the medium of the epiphany. Though what we also learn from reading closely is that there's a large contradiction embedded in the genre, a potentially scandalous one, that both Oprah and James Frey end up wrestling with, each in their own ways.*

The Mind-Body Problem

Oprah's special genius, and the reason we let her play the cultural role she does, is that her problems do so often encapsulate

---

*For someone with so much cultural visibility, it's remarkable how scandal-insulated Oprah has been. When a man named Randolph Cook, who alleged he was her former boyfriend, self-published his own recovery memoir, titled *The Wizard of O: My Life with Oprah*, in 2008, claiming that Oprah had taught him how to smoke crack and that the two had freebased regularly during their six-month romance in the mid-1980s, it barely caused a flutter, except in the *National Enquirer*. In Cook's version, Oprah wrecked his life; he'd obviously like a share of her billions in compensation, though he dropped his $20 million lawsuit against her after a series of motions and counter-motions. (According to an appeals court ruling, Oprah herself had revealed on television in 1995 that she'd abused drugs, though she denied ever having been romantically involved with Cook.) The allegations rippled briefly through the celebrity gossip blogosphere, but the mainstream media kept a wide berth and the story soon faded away. The question of why certain potential scandals fail to scandalize is as mysterious as dogs that don't bark in the night. In this case, Oprah had already admitted the drug abuse, it was well in the past, she has vast media influence (which is why commercial publishers wouldn't touch the book, charged Cook), and an impressive track record of worldwide philanthropy, but the bottom line is that there just didn't seem to be sufficient collective animus to keep the story alive.

the dilemmas of the self in our times, which is why her plaintive question "How did I let this happen again?" can't be read as just a throwaway line; it's worth some serious thought. Essentially it reformulates the epistemological conundrum that's preoccupied philosophers for centuries: How can the self know itself? How can the self ever know what it knows? These aren't unfamiliar questions, they're the central dilemmas of human consciousness, the founding problems of the philosophy of mind. Oprah may frame them in the idioms of addiction and self-help, but lodged between the recovery clichés there's a deeper story about the inherently rickety status of self-knowledge, one that, ironically, threatens to undermine the whole therapeutic project that Oprah's built her career on. Let's call this threat the *self-knowledge lag*.

By *self-knowledge lag*, what I mean is this. When Oprah poses questions like, "What am I really hungry for?" and answers, "I'm hungry for balance, I'm hungry to do something other than work," given the slightness of these insights, you wonder why she couldn't have just figured all this out before, back when she was gaining all the weight. The most obvious reason is that in a narrative structured around a revelation, the revelation can't occur before the denouement. If self-knowledge is modeled as a "journey," then the epiphany can only occur *later*, after the fact. In other words, the built-in paradox of the recovery genre is that self-knowledge *has* to be incomplete; otherwise say goodbye to uphill battles, farewell to relapses and turning points— too much self-acuity, and your story will be excessively brief or, far worse from a publishing standpoint, nonexistent altogether.

But if the therapeutic narrative invariably traces a journey from blindness to epiphany, from self-ignorance to growth, and it's the author's failure to have known something crucial about himself—how to get sober, leave a bad marriage, break some self-destructive pattern—that generates the story, how can an author simultaneously confess to large gaps in self-understanding *and* know himself thoroughly enough to know he's not *still* in the dark, even now? If self-knowledge is perpetually incomplete, because the revealing epiphanies can come only after the fact, doesn't the memoirist have to assume that whatever truth she's constructing *now*, in the present moment, is also incomplete and may eventually be revealed as faulty by yet another epiphany? If you were lying to yourself back then, a victim of insufficient self-knowledge, why think you're so on top of things now?

The requirement to not understand relevant things about oneself and realize them only later would seem to directly contradict the demand that memoirists adhere to juridical standards of truth. After all, the act of writing itself is taking place now, in the present tense, meaning that what you're writing, and the self-knowledge being employed in the writing, can only ever be disastrously partial. Yet, isn't it also this very failure of self-understanding that engages readers in these authors' plights, that makes their stories feel *real* to the rest of us not-completely-self-knowledgeable selves? They share their pain and screw-ups, their arduous paths to self-realization; we buy their books and watch their TV shows, because unfortunately we recognize the condition. It's our shared bond. Yes, there's an underlying incoherence at the core of the connection, but this incoherence is what it is to be human. Or to put it slightly differently, Oprah's weight problem is the most genuine thing about her exactly because, try as she does, she *can't* come up with a coherent narrative about it: it's her thyroid, it's lack of self-care, it's a food addiction—she doesn't *know* what it is.

As we've seen, this not-knowing, the no-man's land where intemperance reigns and incoherence is boss, can't be so easily harnessed to therapeutic narratives: it's disruptive, a holdout, it doesn't *want* to be redeemed. Exhibit A: Frey's literary excesses. Exhibit B: Oprah's excess poundage—excesses where self-knowledge goes to die, where facts and diets spin out of control, a murky realm not unlike what the maddening Slovenian social philosopher Slavoj Zizek calls the Real, though he probably means something different than the "real" of reality TV or the supposed factuality of memoirs. Zizek likes telling an old Soviet-era joke to describe what he does mean. A Jew named Rabinovitch is being interrogated by an emigration official about why he wants to leave the Soviet Union. He has two reasons, Rabinovitch says, the first being that he's afraid Communism will be overthrown and the Jews will get the blame for what the Communists have done. The official assures him that this is ridiculous since Communist power is going to last forever. "Well," responds Rabinovitch, "that's my second reason."

The point is that having two reasons that absolutely contradict each other may just be the only mode of being, our general plight. Genres that hinge on producing self-coherence in readily marketable forms are bound to reproduce this plight—yet that's the most authentic thing about them. It's probably the most authentic form of authenticity around, yet on encountering it Frey's readers felt irreparably damaged, they wanted their money back! If recovery lit turns out to contain the seeds of its own unraveling, this would seem to put it in the neighborhood of Zizek's Real, something unfathomable and uncanny that can't be directly represented, though it emerges between the cracks—in jokes, for instance, or in the contradictions of mass culture, such as the recovery genre's demand to both *not* know something crucial about yourself yet *also* adhere strictly to the truth. Whatever moral there is to be distilled from this murk, it's in the symbolic deadlock itself, in the impossibility of meeting such a demand.

If people routinely fail to tell the truth about themselves, all the while announcing what honest characters they are— well, the truth is that you *can* both know something and not know it at the same time. You can look down and realize you've gained forty pounds without quite having "realized" it even though your pants won't zip; maybe you can even confess to invented crimes without quite "realizing" how far you've gone, then confess to having invented the previous confession in a final act of Telling It Like It Is. Sadly, the same goes for all of us, armed with our tardy self-realizations and over-defensive certainties.

Epiphanies Inc.

Speaking of self-knowledge lags: it was reported in the press and confirmed by an Oprah representative that in fall 2008, two and a half years after their televised face-off, Oprah phoned James Frey to apologize for what she'd put him through during the show. In what was billed as "an astonishing, self-reflective call" by *Vanity Fair*, which broke the story, Oprah told Frey that at the time she'd felt betrayed but that she now realized her harsh evisceration of him had been coming, unfairly, from her own ego. She'd had an epiphany that morning while meditating.

No one wants to begrudge Oprah her epiphanies, however belated (epiphanies can *only* be belated), though of course we also deeply enjoy bashing other people for their failures of timely insights and all the abysmal clichés they come up with to paper over the gaps. Even Frey has been known to play the bad cop on this when given the chance, ranting at one point in *A Million Little Pieces* about "a famous Rock Star who was once a Patient here," who visited Frey's rehab facility to deliver a preening testimonial about recovery. Frey's actually quite funny on the subject: "He talks about living on the road and says it ain't easy, man, even if you are staying at the Four Seasons." The posturing peeves Frey, as does the Rock Star's claim about the immense quantities of drugs and alcohol he'd consumed in his day, which have to be fantasies and exaggerations, Frey thinks. (Obviously that competitive streak wasn't confined to other writers!) If he were in his normal frame of mind, he says, he'd stand up, point my finger, scream Fraud, and chase this Chump Motherfucker down and give him a beating, I would make him come back here and apologize to everyone for wasting their precious time. After the apology, I would tell him that if I ever heard of him spewing his bullshit fantasies in Public again, I would cut off his precious hair, scar his precious lips, and take all of his goddamned gold records and shove them straight up his ass.

His grievance is that bragging about being an addict or reveling in the mock glory of it isn't in any way related to the *truth*, "and that is all that matters, the truth." Needless to say, accusations about bullshit fantasies would soon be turned on Frey himself: subsequent events make this passage read like a proleptic self-indictment. Maybe that was the point.

Self-indictments are a hot item at the moment. Confessing to substance problems and other self-management failures may be our culture's version of authenticity, but it's also kitsch, our rendition of sad clowns painted on black velvet. Authenticity is a brand, recovery narratives our Muzak. Why call them kitsch? Because kitsch is the attempt to have your emotions on the cheap. The problem with the ascendancy of the therapeutic narrative as a cultural form isn't just the commodified authenticity, it's the sentimentality in place of deep feeling, the pseudo-catharsis soothing and appeasing the audience. Remember, you too have untapped depths, it tells us, even if the depths are packaged in easy-to-swallow doses, reducing every conflict and need to a handful of cheesy formulas. The big, showy emotions performed before audiences in the millions are the media age's equivalent of classic kitsch's iconic single tear rolling down a cheek—engineered for maximum effect and striving to please, as kitsch always does.

But this is our cultural situation, and we all know it. It's the economic deal we've struck, ambivalent though we may occasionally be. We know the sentiments are mass produced, we also know the emotions we need to sustain us can't be packaged, yet with the Oprahfication of the culture, triteness is our fate: it saturates the culture and our lives. What's at issue isn't the market or mass media, neither of which appear to be going away anytime soon, it's the flattening out of experience and the vacancies it leaves all of us to manage, each in our own improvised ways. If every scandal exposes underlying social contradictions, the commerce in selfhood is the subtext of this one. The question we'd want to ask is whether her talent at monetizing authenticity really gives Oprah the moral high ground over James Frey. Recall that for critics like Kakutani, it was their similarities that drove this scandal, even though Oprah is clearly the more adept practitioner of the form.

Frey's real crime was shining a spotlight on the inherent unreliability of a vastly commercial and vastly popular genre and exposing the duplicities haunting its core, beginning with the fact that the warm glow of authenticity they generate is a literary effect. Even the most compelling memoirs are artifice, not truth; they're words on a page. The epiphanies wielded by the authors are provisional at best, contrivances at worst. Or to put it in functional terms, they're necessitated by the structure of the genre, a product of the recovery story's narrative machinery. From this standpoint, Frey wasn't a liar, he was the consummate (if inadvertent) truth teller—yet another thing to hold against him.

As with scandals generally: they tell us things we didn't want to know, for instance that the unreliable narrator isn't a literary device alone, it's an ontological condition. Ha ha. And this, I suspect, is basically what scandal is up to: it's *mocking* us. Its greatest delight is making garish public spectacles out of our internal miasma, giving us an externalized portrait of the structure of the psyche itself. As if anyone really wanted to know!

Frey added a new section to the paperback edition of his subsequent book, *Bright Shiny Morning* (this one was marketed as a novel), about a writer who, having been publicly disgraced by a talk show host and no longer trusting anyone, begins taping all his phone calls. Thus the tape recorder is running when the talk show host phones the writer soon after a devastating appearance on her show because she's worried he's going to hurt himself. They talk for almost an hour; she says many things that contradict her public statements; she tells him embarrassing things about her life before she was famous and all the mistakes she's made. "He taped everything," Frey writes, adding, "Someday he might tell his side of it. Someday he might play the tapes. Someday."

And does Frey have a stash of secret tapes hidden away somewhere of a famous talk show host confessing embarrassing things, or is he toying with us again? Could there be another scandal around the corner? Of course there is—if not this one, an even better one.

EPILOGUE

One of the obvious impediments to writing—by which I mean *completing*—a book on scandal is the unending barrage of material, coupled with the rapid exhaustion rate of the example pool. Are you going to include this new scandal or that one, everyone you know queries so "helpfully" every time another ingénue self-implodes or the latest billion-dollar Ponzi scheme is exposed, until the prospective manuscript starts to resemble one of those Borges stories about the infinite book with the indefinite number of pages containing every known instance and scrap of information relating to its ostensible subject with no beginning or end, driving author, readers, and librarians to states of suicidal despair. Additionally, scandal conditions keep shifting under our feet: many things that were scandalous fifty years ago now aren't (illegitimacy, interracial marriage), various things that weren't scandalous then now are (middle-aged women seducing teenage boys, white comedians berating black hecklers with the word "nigger"), and with the rise of confessional culture, shame just isn't what it used to be.

At the same time, could there be a more effortless subject? You're going around minding your own business, and these split-off fragments of other people's repressions and wishes come hurtling at you from the social ether like messages in a bottle, one bedeviled psyche flagging down another, demanding to be deciphered. Maybe I have a special affinity for these knotted little stories because writing and scandal have certain similarities, poised as writers often are between the murky chasms of unknowingness and whatever thin protections against it form or style provide (so you hope).

Or perhaps I'm over-dwelling on the writing-scandal kinship—as everyone knows, writers are prone to excess identification with their subjects, often to the point of monomania. I'm reminded here of Joyce Carol Oates's forward to her admirably short book *On Boxing*, which opens with the largish claim that "no other subject is, for the writer, so intensely personal as boxing. To write about boxing is to write about oneself—however elliptically, and unintentionally." A bit further on she completely reverses herself: "The writer contemplates his opposite in the boxer." So which is it, self or opposite? I suspect the answer is both, though you see how much coherence even the sharpest of writers brings to the topic of the self and its projections, which is worrisome to those of us plowing in the same pasture. Not to pick a fight with the estimable Oates over the autobiographical valances of our respective subjects, but if writing on boxing lets bookish neurasthenic types identify with aggression and love their inner brutes, surely scandal thrusts a writer into even more intensely personal and less safely elliptical terrain, riddled with compulsion, neurosis, grandiosity, and a thousand other unflattering propensities. Additionally, as we've seen, writers themselves have demonstrated a remarkable talent for scandal-courting lately: inventing ordeals, faking facts, swiping each other's stuff—all of which no doubt seemed like a good idea at the time, but then the tendency to mistake bad ideas for good ones is exactly the thing you never see in yourself until it's too late, like some asymptomatic disease you don't know you have until suddenly you're covered in pustules and everyone's inching away.

But let me cut the self-inspection short—having spent the majority of this book enumerating its limits, it would be a little self-contradictory to rely on it now. Of course, self-contradiction *is* pandemic. It's the universal human scourge and there's no known cure—the most prevalent disability on the planet, yet where are the telethons and charity auctions for *these* uncounted victims? Which leads me to a final point. If a tabloid society's attention is trained on the gutter instead of the mountaintops and heavens, it's not just out of prurience or for the sheer malevolent fun of it (though there's always that). It's that scandal, even in its most minor forms, even the small-bore violations worth no more than a squib on page 22—the top White House domestic policy adviser picked up for shoplifting in a suburban discount chain store after trying to return the shoplifted goods for cash, the university president forced to resign his post after making a series of obscene phone calls from his own office phone (isn't this something a practical-minded obscene phone caller would prefer to do from a phone booth?)—reveals something true about the human situation, truer than the usual truisms. To begin with, there's the not inconsiderable contradiction that on the one hand we struggle to survive (so the prevailing theory goes), yet there's this prodigious talent for self-destruction. On the one hand a sufficient quotient of self-awareness is necessary for social survival, yet self-awareness is such a faulty product there should be a universal recall.

The function of scandal is a complicated business, to say the least. Maybe there's been so little inquisitiveness about the nature of these complications—what I've called the psychodynamics of scandal—because too much awareness raises too many questions. On the plus side, other people's foibles make us feel better about our own. Additionally, scandal offers ways of organizing the collectivity's hatred, which can't be so easily crystallized around the traditional targets these days (blacks and Jews have gotten testy about playing that part). As scandal reveals, the social world is in an eternal search for scapegoats. This makes it a brutal place, to be sure, but the scapegoat process *is* intrinsic to every social group. Societies have always purified themselves through shows of moral indignation, dumping their burdens off onto designated candidates—all the abnormality and moral disability that threatens to poison the community. Those cast in this unlucky role don't have to be innocent victims either; a scapegoat's crimes can be entirely real.* If it's the scandalizer's fate to enact the self-sabotaging tendencies that vex the human personality, then what better sacrificial figure?

Living in a group is the basic human challenge: admittance is conditional and the threat of exile perpetually looms. At any moment you can be kicked out on your ass simply for being clumsy at the social adaptation business, which doesn't always come easily given the self-awareness problem. And the endless prohibitions, both written and unwritten. Consider the intricacies of the various transgressions detailed in the preceding pages—how would you begin to teach someone all these rules if forced to enumerate them? *"Don't tape-record the phone conversations of your girlfriend who happens to be having an affair with the president." "Don't impersonate a private detective from Texas and stalk your ex-lover." "Don't get suspected of urinating into diapers in your car while on a deranged road trip to Orlando." "Don't exaggerate."* But what a kettle of creativity too, as if something antic in the makeup of the human animal were thumbing its nose at conventions and limits, lobbying the world to conform to *it*, instead of the other way around. You can almost hear scandal scoffing, "Shove your rules!" and I suspect that in a secret corner deep within every upright overly-socialized outwardly compliant citizen,

---

*Criminals have always made excellent scapegoats.

there's some tiny recalcitrant element that would like to agree.

Typically, the social world wins such contests. If the self were in any way transparent to itself things might be otherwise, but as we see, unconsciousness circulates as invisibly as a virus. Despite the brutality of the deterrents, scandal thrives; in fact, new candidates are queuing even now, just waiting for the nod. All that's required is a lapse of self-knowledge (pretty much the human condition), the right opportunity (not that difficult to arrange), a few errant desires (who doesn't want more of *something*, hungry babyish selves that we are?), and you're in business.

But don't worry, it will never be *you* in the stew, savaged in the media, life in a million little pieces. And hopefully not me. But it's definitely going to be someone, since when has there been a scandal-free age? Never!

BIBLIOGRAPHY

A Note on Sources

The basic facts in these cases are on the public record; all were widely reported as the scandals unfolded. The narratives and inferences are based on the mainstream press coverage and other published sources; I haven't interviewed any of the principals. It bears mentioning that in most of the cases, at least some of the facts are in dispute; where relevant, I've mentioned those disputes. (Though as I also say somewhere along the way, scandals don't have to be *true* to be scandalous.) The news reports are available online and I've indicated some of the locations below for anyone who wants to go back to the original sources. I've also listed other reportage I've consulted and some of the texts that influenced my general thinking about scandal, or the specifics of these cases.

Bibliography

Introduction

There's been only one previous book about scandal as a general subject, Ari Adut's *On Scandal: Moral Disturbances in Society, Politics, and Art*, Cambridge: Cambridge University Press, 2008, though Adut, a sociologist, takes a very different vantage from mine, examining scandal primarily from the standpoint of social structures and institutions.

Brooks, Peter. *Troubling Confessions: Speaking Guilt in Law and Literature.* Chicago: University of Chicago Press, 2000.

Burke, Kenneth. *Language as Symbolic Action: Essays on Life, Literature, and Method.* Berkeley: University of California Press, 1966.

Freud, Sigmund. *Civilization and Its Discontents.* 1930. Translated and reprinted in *Standard Edition*, vol. 21, London: Hogarth, 1961, 59–148.

———. "Fragment of an Analysis of a Case of Hysteria." 1905. Translated and reprinted in *Standard Edition*, vol. 7, London: Hogarth, 1961, 64–94 (see ch. 2, "The First Dream").

———. "From the History of an Infantile Neurosis." 1918: part 4. Translated and reprinted in *Standard Edition*, vol. 17 (see "The Dream and the Primal Scene," 29–47).

Geertz, Clifford. "Deep Play: Notes on the Balinese Cockfight." *The Interpretation of Cultures.* New York: Basic, 2000.

Hyde, Lewis. *Trickster Makes This World: Mischief, Myth, and Art.* New York: North Point, 1998.

Polti, Georges. *The Thirty-Six Dramatic Situations.* 1921. Translated by Lucille Ray. Boston: The Writer, Inc., 1977.

Strachey, James. *Eminent Victorians.* 1918. London: Penguin, 1986.

Wolf, Naomi. "Sex and Silence at Yale." *New York*, March 1, 2004.

Chapter 1 The Lovelorn Astronaut

The story was covered most thoroughly in the *Orlando Sentinel*; its Web site, orlandosentinel.com, also posted the prison footage of

Nowak, transcripts of the police interviews, Nowak's press conference, and the televised courtroom footage of various legal motions and proceedings.

Carey, Benedict. "Stumbling Blocks on the Path of Righteousness." *New York Times*, May 5, 2009.

Coetzee, J. M. "Confession and Double Thoughts: Tolstoy, Rousseau, Dostoevsky." *Comparative Literature 37* (Summer 1985): 193–232.

Elias, Norbert. *The History of Manners.* 1939. Translated by Edmund Jephcott. New York: Pantheon, 1978.

Fanning, Diane. *Out There: The In-Depth Story of the Astronaut Love Triangle That Shocked America.* New York: St. Martin's, 2007.

Fingarette, Herbert. *Self-Deception.* 1969. Berkeley: University of California Press, 2000.

Gergen, Kenneth. *The Saturated Self: Dilemmas of Identity in Contemporary Life.* New York: Basic, 1991.

Hollandsworth, Skip. "Suburban Madness." *Texas Monthly*, November 2002.

Leach, Colin Wayne. "Malicious Pleasure: Schadenfreude at the Suffering of Another Group." *Journal of Personality and Social Psychology* 84 (2003): 932–43.

Mackenzie, Margaret A. *Courting the Media: Public Relations for the Accused and the Accuser.* New York: Praeger, 2007.

Reik, Theodor. "Forgiveness and Vengeance." *The Compulsion to Confess: On the Psychoanalysis of Crime and Punishment.* New York: Grove, 1945.

Trilling, Diana. *Mrs. Harris: The Death of the Scarsdale Diet Doctor.* New York: Penguin, 1981.

Wolfe, Tom. *The Right Stuff.* New York: Farrar, Straus and Giroux, 1979.

Chapter 2 An Unreasonable Judge

The story was reported as it unfolded in the *New York Times*. Those articles are available online, beginning with the Wachtler-Cuomo face-off in October 1991, continuing though Wachtler's arrest in November 1992, with regular updates on the case until his sentencing in March 1993.

Briles, Judith. *Stop Stabbing Yourself in the Back: Zapping the Enemy Within.* Aurora, CO: Mile High Press, 2002.

Brooks, Peter, and Paul Gewirtz, eds. *Law's Stories: Narrative and Rhetoric in the Law.* New Haven: Yale University Press, 1998.

Caher, John M. *King of the Mountain: The Rise, Fall, and Redemption of Chief Judge Sol Wachtler.* Amherst, NY: Prometheus, 1998.

Crotty, Kevin M. *Law's Interior: Legal and Literary Constructions of the Self.* Ithaca: Cornell University Press, 2001.

Franks, Lucinda. "The Judge and I." *New York,* November 14, 1994, 40–46.

———. "To Catch a Judge: How the F.B.I. Tracked Sol Wachtler." *New Yorker,* December 21, 1992, 58–66.

Freud, Sigmund. "Psychoanalytic Notes upon an Autobiographical Account of a Case of Paranoia; or, The Psychotic Doctor Schreber." 1911. In *Three Case Histories.* Ed. Philip Rieff. New York: Macmillan, 1963.

"Judge Not" [interview with Sol Wachtler]. *Psychology Today,* July–August 1997.

Reik, Theodor. *The Compulsion to Confess: On the Psychoanalysis of Crime and Punishment.* New York: Grove, 1945.

———. *Masochism in Modern Man.* Translated by Margaret H. Beigel and Gertrud M. Kurth. New York: Grove, 1941.

Santner, Eric L. *My Own Private Germany: Daniel Paul Schreber's Secret History of Modernity.* Princeton: Princeton University Press, 1996.

Schreber, Daniel Paul. *Memoirs of My Nervous Illness.* Ed. Rosemary Dinnage. New York: New York Review of Books, 2000.

Wachtler, Sol. *After the Madness: A Judge's Own Prison Memoir.* New York: Random House, 1997.

Wolfe, Linda. *Double Life: The Shattering Affair between Chief Judge*

Sol Wachtler and Socialite Joy Silverman. New York: Pocket Books, 1994.

Chapter 3 The Whistle-Blower

Those seeking additional details on Tripp's role in the Clinton impeachment will want to consult Jeffrey Toobin's *A Vast Conspiracy: The Real Story of the Sex Scandal That Nearly Brought Down a President*, New York: Random House, 1999. There's also Andrew Morton's *Monica's Story*, New York: St. Martin's, 1999. Of some interest is a vituperative 1998 online debate between *Time*'s Margaret Carlson and Lucianne Goldberg's son, Jonah, now a well-known conservative columnist, on the subject of Tripp's betrayals and her appearance (http://www.slate.com/id/3681/entry/24114/). As for other aspects of the argument, I discuss the woman-disgust connection more extensively in the chapter on "Dirt" in my previous book, *The Female Thing: Dirt, Envy, Sex, Vulnerability*, New York: Pantheon, 2006; there's a longer bibliography on the subject there.

Bloom, Harold. *Shakespeare: The Invention of the Human*. New York: Riverhead, 1998.

Canetti, Elias. *Crowds and Power*. 1960. Translated by Carol Stewart. New York: Farrar, Straus and Giroux, 1984.

Cole, Jonathan. *About Face*. Cambridge: MIT Press, 1998.

Cousins, Mark. "The Ugly." *AA Files* 28 (1996): 61–64; *AA Files* 29 (1996).

Ekman, Paul, ed. *Emotion in the Human Face*. Cambridge: Cambridge University Press, 1984.

Foucault, Michel. *Discipline and Punish: The Birth of the Prison*. Translated by Alan Sheridan. New York: Vintage, 1979.

Freud, Sigmund. *Jokes and Their Relation to the Unconscious*. Translated by James Strachey. New York: Norton, 1963.

Gilman, Sander L. *Creating Beauty to Cure the Soul: Race and Psychology in the Shaping of Aesthetic Surgery*. Durham: Duke University Press, 1998.

Goffman, Erving. *Stigma: Notes on the Management of Spoiled Identity.* New York: Simon and Schuster, 1963.

Kant, Immanuel. *Critique of Judgment.* Translated by J. H. Bernard. New York: Haffner, 1951.

Kris, Ernst. *Psychoanalytic Explorations in Art.* New York: International Universities Press, 1952.

Kubie, Lawrence S. "The Fantasy of Dirt." *Psychoanalytic Quarterly* 6 (1937): 388–425.

Mayer, Jane. "For the Record." *New Yorker,* June 8, 1998, 34–36.

————. "Portrait of a Whistleblower." *New Yorker,* March 23, 1998, 34–47.

Miller, William Ian. *The Anatomy of Disgust.* Cambridge: Harvard University Press, 1997.

Moore, Ronald. "Ugliness." In *Encyclopedia of Aesthetics.* Vol. 4. Edited by Michael Kelly. New York: Oxford University Press, 1998.

Rozin, Paul. "The Borders of the Self: Contamination Sensitivity and Potency of the Body Apertures and Other Body Parts." *Journal of Research in Personality* 29 (1995): 318–40.

Rozin, Paul, Laura Lowery, and Rhonda Ebert. "Varieties of Disgust Faces and the Structure of Disgust." *Journal of Personality and Social Psychology* 66 (1994): 870–81.

Sedgwick, Eve, and Adam Frank, eds. *Shame and Its Sisters: A Silvan Tomkins Reader.* Durham: Duke University Press, 1995.

Stolnitz, Jerome. "Ugliness." In *Encyclopedia of Philosophy.* Vol. 8. Edited by Paul Edward. New York: Macmillan, 1967.

Synnott, Anthony. "Truth and goodness, mirrors and masks: a sociology of beauty and the face, Parts I and II." *British Journal of Sociology* 40, no. 4 (1989); 41, no. 1 (1990).

Tomkins, Silvan S. *Affect, Imagery, Consciousness.* Vol. 1. New York: Springer, 1962.

Walsh, Anthony. "The Holy Trinity and the Legacy of the Italian School of Criminal Anthropology." *Human Nature Review* 3 (2003): 1–11.

Chapter 4 An Over-imaginative Writer

This story was reported so extensively it's hard to know where to start as far as sources. The first place to look would be the Smoking Gun story ("A Million Little Lies: Exposing James Frey's Fiction Addiction," www.thesmokinggun.com, January 8, 2006), as well as the material on Frey available on Oprah's Web site (www.oprah.com). Evgenia Peretz's *Vanity Fair* stories, cited below, are also informative. Frey himself often discussed the scandal while publicizing his 2008 novel; you can watch various interviews with him on the subject on YouTube.

Barthes, Roland. "The Death of the Author." *Image-Music-Text.* Translated by Stephen Heath. New York: Hill and Wang, 1977.

Barton, Linda. "The Man Who Rewrote His Life." *The Guardian*, September 15, 2006, G6.

Cook, L. Randolph. *The Wizard of O: My Life with Oprah.* All Means Necessary Publishing, 2007.

Frank, Thomas. "Shocked, Shocked! Enronian Myths Exploded." *Nation*, April 8, 2002.

Frey, James. *Bright Shiny Morning.* New York: Harper, 2008.

———. *A Million Little Pieces.* New York: Doubleday, 2003.

———. *My Friend Leonard.* New York: Riverhead, 2005.

Gates, Henry Louis Jr. "'Authenticity,' or the Lesson of Little Tree." *New York Times Book Review*, November 24, 1991.

Greenberg, Clement. "Avant-Garde and Kitsch." *Partisan Review* 6, no. 5 (1939): 34–49.

Harris, Paul. "You Go, Girl." *The Observer* (London), November 20, 2005, 27.

Hart, Francis R. "Notes for an Anatomy of Modern Autobiography." *New Literary History* 1 (Spring 1970): 485–511.

Illouz, Eva. *Oprah Winfrey and the Glamour of Misery: An Essay on Popular Culture.* New York: Columbia University Press, 2003.

Kakutani, Michiko. "Bending the Truth in a Million Little Ways." *New York Times*, January 17, 2006.

Lasch, Christopher. *The Culture of Narcissism: American Life in an Age of Diminishing Expectations.* New York: Norton, 1979.

Lazar, David, ed. *Truth in Nonfiction.* Iowa City: University of Iowa Press, 2008.

Lejune, Philippe. *On Autobiography.* Translated by Katherine Leary. Minneapolis: University of Minnesota Press, 1989.

Otis, Ginger Adams. "Oprah's Painful Years." *New York Post.* May 27, 2007.

Peretz, Evgenia. "James Frey Gets a Bright Shiny Apology from Oprah." *VanityFair.com,* May 11, 2009.

———. "James Frey's Morning After." *Vanity Fair,* June 2008, 140–72.

Rich, Frank. "Tiger Woods, Person of the Year." *New York Times,* December 20, 2009.

Schiffrin, André. *The Business of Books: How the International Conglomerates Took Over Publishing and Changed the Way We Read.* New York: Verso, 2001.

Scruton, Roger. "Kitsch and the Modern Predicament." *City Journal,* Winter 1999.

Traig, Jennifer, ed. *The Autobiographer's Handbook.* New York: Henry Holt, 2008.

Weber, Max. *The Protestant Ethic and the Spirit of Capitalism.* Translated by Talcott Parsons. New York: Charles Scribner's Sons, 1958.

Winfrey, Oprah. "How Did I Let This Happen Again?" *O: The Oprah Magazine,* January 2009.

Zizek, Slavoj. *The Sublime Object of Ideology.* New York: Verso, 1989.

Epilogue

Girard, René. *The Scapegoat.* Translated by Yvonne Freccero. Baltimore: Johns Hopkins University Press, 1989.

Oates, Joyce Carol. *On Boxing.* New York: Ecco, 1994.

ACKNOWLEDGMENTS

It was my friend Bruce Robbins who convinced me to return to this book, which I'd put aside in frustration, half finished, for years (then wrote a different book about another hair-tearing subject instead); thank you, Bruce, for the adamancy. I'm grateful to Valerie Monroe for many things, including disagreeing with me eloquently on occasion about aspects of my argument. Conversations with Mark Buchan about names, fate, desire, and other classical matters excited my thinking about scandal. Various aperçus by the brilliant George Prochnik have somehow found their way into this book unattributed, sorry! Discussions about previous incarnations of the manuscript with the infinitely kind Eric Chinski at FSG were most useful. My dad, Len Kipnis, read every word of every chapter in multiple drafts: my staunchest reader. Thanks again to Beth Vesel, my agent, for being so great during the many peregrinations of this book. And now we come to my editor, Sara Bershtel, a whirlwind of insight and hilarity. Words alone don't convey the enormousness of my gratitude: I hereby propose marriage. Raves also to Riva Hocherman at Metropolitan, another shrewd cookie, for such deft editorial ministrations. Thanks to Roslyn Schloss, Elliot Jurist, and David Hirshey. And thank you, especially, to Jim Livingston.

ILLUSTRATION CREDITS

Photographs on pages 5, 57, 65, 74, 87, 104, and 115 appear by permission of AP/Wide World Photos; 18, 26, and 163 courtesy of Thesmokinggun.com (thanks to Andrew Goldberg); 27 and 31 from NASA publicity photos; and 69 from the New York State Court of Appeals.

ABOUT THE AUTHOR

LAURA KIPNIS is the author of *Against Love: A Polemic* and *The Female Thing: Dirt, Sex, Envy, Vulnerability*, which have been translated into fourteen languages. She is a professor in the Department of Radio/TV/Film at Northwestern University, has received fellowships from the Guggenheim Foundation, the Rockefeller Foundation, and the National Endowment for the Arts, and has contributed to *Slate, Harper's, The Nation, Playboy*, and *The New York Times Magazine*. She lives in New York and Chicago.